Discovering Jesus

Discovering Jesus

A SELF-STUDY WORKBOOK

Ronnie L Worsham

Copyright © 2015 Ronnie L Worsham
All rights reserved.

ISBN: 1516942434
ISBN 13: 9781516942435

Cover by Matt Clark

To the Lord Jesus Christ

Special Thanks

To Brent Adams:
Brent is the man who taught me the foundational principles of the Bible and helped me develop an abiding love of God's Word. He is the man who taught me the basics that comprise the original outline of this book. He baptized me. He was the one I first caught a love of Jesus from. He was one of the first men of God who ever believed in me. Brent is the man who taught me to love the lost and the hurting and who taught me to preach. He taught me about Christian marriage, and he officiated my wedding to my beautiful wife, Tana. I have only grown to appreciate his love and faith more and more over the years, as I daily use the spirit and the tools that he helped instill in me some forty years ago now. Brent helped build in me the foundation of Jesus Christ, and I owe him greatly and am more thankful for him every day.

Appreciation

To the dedicated leaders and members of the DFW Metro Family of Churches who for the last eighteen years have explored together with me what it means to discover and to help others to discover Jesus. Particular thanks is given to the senior pastors of the five major communities that presently comprise this family of churches, who have led in a collective vision and who have assisted to varying degrees over the years in the development of this material—John Von Runnen, Wylie Northeast Church; Dr. Brad Davis, Denton North Church; Brandon Worsham, Fellowship of Christian University Students (FOCUS), and Dr. Alan Pickering, North Texas Pastoral Counseling Center and Ultimate Life Ministries. I thank the shepherds of the Northeast Church, Dannye Welch, Jack Worsham, and John McWilliams, as well as the shepherds of all of our communities, for their love for our fellowship and for shepherding a family of churches that has from its very beginning been singly focused on discovering and following Jesus. Thanks are also extended to the members of the Northeast 2020 Leadership team and the Discovering Jesus class who helped in this project by working through the lessons, teaching the lessons, editing material, and providing valuable feedback. I also thank the untold numbers of individuals whom I have taught the various versions and arrangements of this material over the last forty-two years. I have surely learned from each and every one of you. Most of all I thank Jesus Christ, whom we all seek to fully discover.

Contents

	Instructions—Ideas for Using This Material	xiii
	Introduction—Discovering Jesus: The Quest for the Best	xv
Lesson 1	The Design and Interpretation of the Bible	1
Lesson 2	Understanding the Inspiration of the Bible	13
Lesson 3	The Story of the Bible	24
Lesson 4	The Problem of Sin	42
Lesson 5	"Jesus is Lord"	66
Lesson 6	Discovering Jesus	75
Lesson 7	Accepting Jesus as Your Lord: Discipleship	100
Lesson 8	Accepting Christ as Your Savior: Faith, Repentance, and Baptism	112
Lesson 9	Living by the Holy Spirit	136
Lesson 10	Reflections on Encountering Christ: Stories of Encounters with Jesus	151
Lesson 11	The Body of Christ, the Church: Living in the Community of Christ	174
Lesson 12	Living as a Christian	190
Lesson 13	Mission and Organization of the Church	219
	Conclusion Moving Forward	237

Instructions—Ideas for Using This Material

This workbook is designed to provide one who wishes to engage in a study of the scope and overall theme of the Bible a way to do so. It is designed to not only allow the student a way to arrive at specific answers from scriptures but also provoke open-minded, objective thinking and questioning. The workbook is divided into thirteen specific lessons; however, by no means is it expected that a student should be able to sit down and complete a lesson in one sitting. In fact, the expectation is quite the contrary. The material should ideally be taken at the student's own pace and taste, allowing for additional research and discussion on topics and questions of particular interest or concern. It should not be a quick study.

The workbook can simply be a self-study guide for one who desires to learn alone. It can also be a group-study guide, allowing individual participants to complete the reading and answer the questions on their own and then come together to discuss additional questions or confusing thoughts and ideas and to consider personal applications.

It is also hoped that many can learn to use the overarching framework of this workbook to help those new to the faith or to the Bible or those who are not already Christians learn about God's plan for the redemption of humanity. This is the plan that flows through the Bible and that culminates with the story of Jesus himself. Followers of Jesus are to be disciples of him—that is, they are to be his students. In Bible language a student is in fact a follower and imitator. Disciples are those who have come to know that Jesus has the words of eternal life. And since God's knowledge and understanding are infinite, one's seeking and studying about him must not end at becoming a Christian or wane over the years as one lives for Christ. Rather, the disciple should be a person who grows in curiosity and interest. Growing disciples should be the ones whose minds constantly become more open, excited, and eager to learn the depth and extent of God's truths. Disciples never assume that "enough" is known or that they are correct about everything. Students of the truth of Christ also grow in humility about what has already been learned and in direct proportion to their knowledge, rather than becoming increasingly prideful about what they might know.

Further, for any of us to facilitate the learning of another of the messages of the Bible, we have to be serious students ourselves. In order for us to lead others to be true students and disciples—ones with open hearts to God and his Word—we must exemplify this necessary attitude. This requires an objective and open-minded approach to God and the scripture. It requires that we lead others to him (Jesus) and not to ourselves. This approach is not designed to produce Christians of any brand save that of Jesus himself.

A facilitative approach to learning is encouraged. With such an approach, new learners are encouraged and allowed to work through segments of the lessons on their own and at their own pace. Meetings should be held regularly (or at least by phone or correspondence) to process the information studied. Questions can be answered, important ideas emphasized and explained, and areas of confusion cleared up. The student, through introspection and personal self-reflection, can take the time to share lessons that were learned. This in itself helps in learning, comprehension, and retention. Through the sharing of their own best discoveries, learners can be encouraged and important messages reinforced.

The goal solely and singly is that each person who uses this workbook in any way does so to more fully discover Jesus—the Pearl of Great Price.

A special note: unless otherwise noted, all quoted scriptures are from the New International Version of the Bible (NIV).

INTRODUCTION
Discovering Jesus: The Quest for the Best

INTRODUCTION

NOTHING IN ALL CREATION is more important, more vital, and more exciting than discovering Jesus for yourself and helping others to do so as well. Jesus has promised to be with and in those who help others to follow him (Matt. 28:20; John 14:23).

Attempting to assemble an outline of scriptures and thoughts to lead others to, or more closely to, Jesus is one of the hardest tasks that can be attempted. First, what must be included is most difficult to discern. Second, what does one dare leave out? The whole Bible is filled with words that point to Jesus.

This study guide is written with great humility, brokenness, and even embarrassment. The human side of this effort falls far short of even an adequate attempt to present the dazzling brilliance of our Lord and Savior and what it means to follow him. However, all human efforts will fall short. Seeing him in his totality will only be accomplished when he finally reveals himself in the end. But until then he has given us himself through the Holy Spirit, and he has given us his Word. And only the living Word of God, empowered by the Holy Spirit of God, is capable of taking words on pages, putting them in the minds of seekers, and allowing readers to discover Jesus. Only an act of God's grace, working through the Spirit and God's Word, can produce within us an adoring, imitating heart for Christ.

The intention in this workbook is that no one will attempt to use this guide as merely an intellectual tool but rather that God will use it to help honest seekers to truly discover Jesus or to grow closer to him. God through Jesus created the world we inhabit for his own purposes. His plan from the beginning was to accomplish his purposes through Christ. Thus we need Christ more than we need our next breath, more than we need food and water, more than anything else in this creation. The assigned mission of Christ's church is to help as many as possible come to this realization in discovering Jesus.

The workbook is divided into thirteen individual lessons. By no means should one expect to finish one lesson in a single setting. In fact, individuals, based on their previous knowledge and ability to move through the material, should set their own pace of study. Some of the answers come right from the text. Some of the answers will be a rewording of the text. And others will be merely opinions of the reader. Some will be impossible to completely answer. The study is designed for both individual and group discovery. It is also designed to be used as a guide for disciples to teach others the Bible and to help them discover Jesus.

May God bless you richly as you discover Jesus for the first time or as you grow in your discovery of him!

LESSON 1
The Design and Interpretation of the Bible

INTRODUCTION

THE WORD "BIBLE" IS THE name Christians gave to the scriptures a long time ago. It simply means "the book." Because of its divine origin, the Bible is recognized by many as the "book of books," or the ultimate book. However, it is not just a single book. The Bible contains sixty-six separate books or documents written over an eighteen-hundred-year span by more than forty authors. It is in fact a window through which we may "see" and understand God much better, because through the Bible God reveals much about himself—his nature, his purposes, and his will. Concerning God's revelation to us, the Bible says:

> In the past God spoke to our ancestors through the prophets at many times and in various ways, but in these last days he has spoken to us by his Son, whom he appointed heir of all things, and through whom also he made the universe. The Son is the radiance of God's glory and the exact representation of his being, sustaining all things by his powerful word. After he had provided purification for sins, he sat down at the right hand of the Majesty in heaven. (Heb. 1:1–3)

God has spoken through the ages in many ways. God has certainly revealed himself from the very beginning through the creation itself (Rom. 1:20). However, his overarching revelation of himself was and is through Jesus, the Son of God. Jesus is the "exact representation" of God in human form. The Bible tells us about all things related to Jesus so we may believe in him and understand what God wants to say to us about him and through him.

That is why this workbook is entitled *Discovering Jesus*. Its purpose is to help you be able to wade through the Bible's writings and thus be able to use it to come to a better understanding of Jesus. And by doing so, you may have a more accurate view of God. Jesus said that he was the only way for men to come to God (John 14:6). By coming to understand God "informationally" (i.e., knowing *about* him), we can be equipped to come to know him experientially in our own places and times—to *know* him.

Let's begin by looking at the whole Bible as a unit. Consider for a moment figure 1 below. Because of the vast scope of material it covers, the figure is obviously very simplistic. But it can help as we drill down to the specifics. Note the window with the two panes. The Old Testament leads us to and prepares us for Jesus. It helps us accept Jesus as Lord. The first book of the Bible, Genesis, tells us that God created the world we live in. It explains that men and women were made in the image of God. It also tells the story of mankind's Fall into sin. In Genesis chapters 2 and 3, we see that mankind had a choice to trust in God ("Tree of Life") or to trust in themselves ("Tree of the Knowledge of Good and Evil"). In making the wrong choice, humanity thus faced the consequences—death. Subsequently God gave a system of right and wrong—the Law of Moses—to the nation of Israel. Their experiences with trying to keep a law in order to be right before God clearly demonstrate the futility of such effort. The painful and bitter experiences we read about in the Old Testament bring to light God's just character. Thus we might think of the Old Testament as revealing God's justice, even though all of God's other traits may also be clearly seen there as well. In Jesus, God proved himself to be both just and merciful. The consequence of sin is death, and in his justice God required that debt to be paid. Death means separation and cessation—separation from the holy God and cessation of life. In this case it was to be both spiritually and ultimately physically. However, God himself took on that death sentence by dying on the cross in our place. The New Testament tells the story of Jesus through four gospel accounts ("gospel" means "good news"). Through them and the subsequent New Testament books, we come to understand how God's mercy was extended to mankind through Christ. We can see in the New Testament that God is also very merciful, while still remaining just. Both virtues—justice and mercy—flow from God's very essence, which is love. John tells us that God is love (1 John 4:8). In Jesus's sacrifice on the cross, we come to understand the whole nature of God.

Figure 1: The Bible Is a Two-Paned Window through Which We Can See God

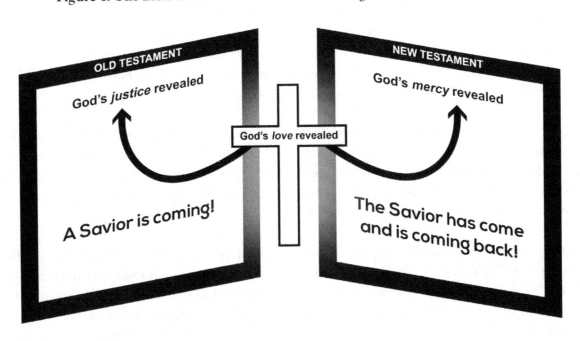

Note: "Testament" is simply another word for "contract" or "covenant."

Consider then: How might seeing the Bible as a window and studying it as such help us see God more clearly?
_____
_____
_____

Question: It is important to see and understand a forest before trying to see and understand the individual trees. Likewise, why is it important for us to see the entire biblical context in order to understand the specific books?
_____
_____
_____

Some basic information about each of the testaments will also be useful in understanding the Bible. Following are lists of general information about each of them that will help in understanding the design of the Bible. There is also an abundance of useful information of all kinds available in books and articles, as well as on the Internet, about the Bible and its parts.

Consider These Old Testament Details:

1. The original manuscripts were written in Hebrew, the language of Israel during Old Testament times.
2. It is widely believed that the first five books were primarily written by Moses. They are also called the "Torah," "The Law," and the "Pentateuch." These are Genesis, Exodus, Leviticus, Numbers, and Deuteronomy.
3. The next twelve books are historical books concerning God's interactions with Israel. These books are Joshua through Esther. Combined, the first seventeen books of the Bible cover the scope of Old Testament history.
4. The next five books are Job, Psalms, Proverbs, Ecclesiastes, and Song of Songs (also known as Song of Solomon). These are books of what is known as wisdom literature, psalms, and poetry. These books were written by and initially to those living during the times written about in the previously mentioned historical books. A proper understanding of the wisdom-literature books requires an understanding of the historical contexts that they derive from and to which they are addressed. It is like trying to understand a speech, such as Abraham Lincoln's "Gettysburg Address." Such a speech requires understanding the issues at that time in history—in this case, mid-nineteenth-century United States, in order to properly understand the speech's original meaning.
5. The last seventeen books of the Old Testament are books of prophecy. In modern times, prophecy is seen as predicting the future. However, the word itself meant "to announce." It has been described as "forthtelling." A true prophet was in effect speaking or announcing for God—giving messages to the people or to individuals directly from God. Peter described prophecy this way: "Prophecy never had its origin in the human will, but prophets, though human, spoke from God as they were carried along by the Holy Spirit" (2 Pet. 1:21). In that they were speaking from God they also were at times able to "foretell" things about the future as revealed to them by God. These last seventeen books are books various prophets of Israel wrote in speaking for God to the people of their day. Thus, understanding more accurately their implications and applications for us in our own times requires understanding them in their original contexts.
6. Isaiah, Jeremiah (who also wrote Lamentations), Ezekiel, and Daniel are often called the "Major Prophets." This is not because they are more important but because they are simply longer documents. The remaining twelve of these books (Hosea through Malachi) are called the "Minor Prophets" because they are considerably shorter. (A special note here: the Bible has been used and written about for thousands of years, and thus, when studying it, you will find it wrapped with old and sometimes antiquated language and descriptions that may not make sense to us today. Therefore, when you study materials about it, especially older material, you will have to do a little extra interpretation of certain words and descriptions that might be used.)
7. As you study the New Testament, depending on your translation, you will find references to "the law and the prophets," "the scriptures," or "the Holy Scriptures." These references are generally to the books of the Old Testament as a whole.

Consider These New Testament Details:

1. The original manuscripts were written primarily in Greek, the most universal language of New Testament times. Outside of the cities in Israel at the time of Jesus, Aramaic was more generally spoken, and therefore in the New Testament, Aramaic words and expressions are to be found.
2. The first four books of the New Testament are Matthew, Mark, Luke, and John. These are called the gospels (meaning "good news"). They tell the story of Jesus's life and ministry as well as important events surrounding them. Mark was a follower of Jesus and was likely the first to put his story into writing. Mark probably collaborated with the apostle Peter in writing this gospel. It was written with the Greco-Roman world at large in mind. Matthew and John were two of Jesus's original twelve apostles. Matthew writes to the Jewish point of view, carefully explaining from Old Testament references that Jesus was indeed the Messiah. (The title "Messiah" comes from the Hebrew and "Christ" from Greek and English. Both mean "king.") Matthew also carefully cataloged all of the core teachings of Christ. John could be considered as the official biographer of Jesus. His book is the last of the four gospels written. It addresses the church at large and is quite personal and insightful. John was the apostle who was considered to be Jesus's closest friend. Luke was a non-Jewish physician who became a disciple of Christ and subsequently was a traveling companion of the apostle Paul. He states that he carefully researched the events surrounding Christ in order to present an orderly account. Paul's knowledge of Jesus is most assuredly reflected in Luke's account. Although the gospels all write an account of Jesus in his lifetime, they were written some thirty to sixty years after his death. Some cast doubt on the gospels' accuracy due to this fact; however, historically speaking, this time frame is amazingly close to the period covered and in fact strengthens their overall historical validity.
3. The book of Acts was written by Luke as a follow-up to his gospel. It further tells a bit about Jesus's time on earth after his resurrection. It then describes the spread of Christianity from Jerusalem to Rome, primarily through the ministries of Peter and Paul. Acts thus gives us a history of some of the earliest churches. It emphasizes the outpouring of the Holy Spirit on the church in chapter 2 and then describes the Spirit's subsequent work in strengthening the church and helping it to fulfill its mission during that time.
4. Next come the "epistles," or more recently called "letters." The word "epistle" is just an older English word for "letter." The first nine of the letters are Romans through 2 Thessalonians. These were letters written by Paul to various churches. As previously mentioned, to understand their true meanings and applications, we must take the time to understand their historical situations and contexts.
5. The next four letters are 1 and 2 Timothy, Titus, and Philemon. These are four letters written by Paul to various individuals. They are often referred to as pastoral letters since they are written to four church leaders. "Pastor" comes from a Greek word meaning "feeder" or "shepherd." Many churches use that term today to describe their primary leader or preacher. "Pastoral" in this case simply means they were written to pastors about pastoring or shepherding the flock of God.
6. Hebrews is a letter to dispersed Jewish Christians, but it is uncertain who the author was. However, no matter who wrote it, during its time it quickly became widely accepted by many of the early churches as part of the authoritative scriptures. "Hebrew" was a term rooted in Israel's history and ultimately became a term outsiders sometimes used to refer to the Israelites. The earlier language of the Jews was also often called Hebrew. Hebrews is a letter encouraging Jewish converts to Christianity to remain true to their commitments to Christ and not to return to the old ways of the Law.

7. James was a letter written by James, who is generally considered the same James who was the biological brother of Jesus. This book is believed by many to be the earliest New Testament book written. It is sometimes called the Proverbs of the New Testament because of the similar way it reads.
8. First and Second Peter are letters written by the apostle Peter. These letters were probably circulated, after the apostle Paul's execution, to the churches that Paul had started through his earlier mission work.
9. First through Third John are letters considered to have been written by the apostle John, who also wrote one of the gospels and traditionally is considered the author of the last book of the New Testament, Revelation. These three letters are brief books of encouragement and admonition.
10. Jude is a letter written by Jude, who along with James is also believed by many to be a biological brother of Jesus.
11. Revelation is called a book of prophecy in that it is revealing and announcing on behalf of God. Either the apostle John or another well-respected church leader named John wrote it. Either way, the early Christians generally accepted it as scripture. It is written in a type of literature called "apocalyptic" (meaning revealing what is hidden). It is a sort of combination of prophecy and poetry in that it reveals God's Word through highly symbolic messages. It is one of the more controversial New Testament books in how it is interpreted. It is a pastoral message letting the early Christians who were being oppressed and persecuted know that Christ will ultimately and definitively win this battle and bring about the culmination of his eternally delivered and redeemed kingdom.

Figure 2 depicts all the books of the Bible in their groupings as if on a bookcase. This allows you to see the Bible writings in the big picture and then to see them broken down into groupings. Many Christians have found it helpful to memorize the books of the Bible in order to be able to move more quickly through them when studying and to be able to mentally place them in their biblical contexts.

Figure 2: The Bible Books and Their Categories

Focusing on God through the Bible

In figure 1, the Bible is described as a window with two panes through which we can look back historically through the Bible writings to see and understand God better. In figure 3, the Bible can also be seen as a lens, the purpose of which is to be able to look deeper into the scriptures to see, find, and come to know God informationally, experientially, and then personally. In order to "get" God out of scripture, we must analyze each layer to understand the context and then "peel back" one layer at a time, taking into consideration the information we have found that is pertinent to effective interpretation. The goal in this process is to finally be able to discern the underlying truths of God at the core. Only by understanding the three outer layers of a book's context and information in sequence and working from the outside in can the scripture be understood in its proper context and thus aptly applied to our current time and contexts.

The figure also reminds us that ultimately Jesus Christ is the "interpretive benchmark" by which God is to be understood. He is the "exact representation of God." Jesus did not just bring the truth; he *is* the truth (John 14:6). Jesus said everyone on the side of the truth listens to him (John 18:37). Every Bible truth is to be understood through the life and teachings of Jesus—how he taught and how he lived it out. Figure 3 depicts the way the Bible lens focuses in on God.

One might also think in terms of the outer three layers comprising the husk of a peanut and the middle as the nutritional substance. The husk is essential to the development and protection of the peanut; however, it is not the tasty, nutritional, and edible part of a peanut. Similarly, the outer layers of the Bible are essential to understanding and finding God, but they are not the ultimate substance we must focus on and find our nourishment in. Remember, the goal is to discover Jesus in scripture so that we can come to God.

Figure 3: Using the Bible as the Lens to Focus in on God

Christ is the "exact representation of God" in human form (Heb. 1:3). Jesus said that when we see him, we see God the Father (John 14:9).

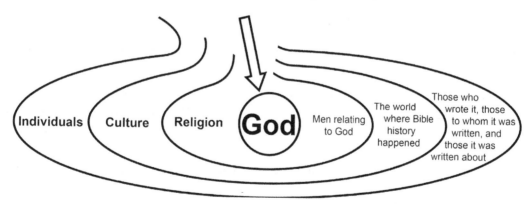

The goal is to find God. We must peel back the layers to find God (John 5:39–40).

The first and most obvious things seen as we read scripture are the viewpoints and thoughts of the writers of the material as well as the perspectives and concerns of the recipients or initial audience of each book. We might, for understanding's sake, call this the layer of the Individuals. Each writer wrote out of his own context speaking into others' contexts. They wrote about what they had seen, had heard about, or had revealed to them by the Holy Spirit. They wrote of mutual interests and concerns they shared with their audiences. Also it is at this layer that the type of literature and writing style being used must be identified as well so that the book can be read and interpreted accordingly. Then too, each book must be considered and interpreted in its greater overall biblical context. This first layer must thus be generally understood in order to develop the intended understanding of what must be learned about God and his purposes that lie beneath it.

The next layer is about the cultural context of what is being written. The revelations and prophecies from God were spoken and written to specific times and contexts. To properly interpret what is being said, a reasonable understanding of the cultures involved is critical. Otherwise, customs of a particular culture or people group, common practices of various countries and societies, and the varied social values that might be implied, as well as manners of speech and idioms, might themselves be seen as binding to all cultures past and present. Making this mistake will actually impede one from seeing the deeper, underlying principles that are to be understood and practiced. In addition the failure to understand cultural contexts can make applications to the present times nonsensical or biblically undesirable.

The final layer to be understood and peeled back involves the religious context. The term "religion" in this case is simply referring to a specific kind of belief system likely involved in any particular scripture's time and place. When Cain and Abel offered sacrifices to God (Gen. 4), they were acting out of their religion or beliefs. When Abraham recognized Melchizedek as a priest and gave a tithe (10 percent) of all the bounty he had just recovered from the raiders, he was acting out of his religion. In some such cases, it is not even known what was behind their practices. God also instructed Israel in a particular set of beliefs and practices under the Law of Moses. Similarly in the New Testament, some writings involve a more Jewish audience and some are written more to the Greco-Roman mind-set. Understanding the belief systems (religions) of the writers and recipients can help us separate a historical set of beliefs and practices from the underlying purposes and meanings found only in God himself.

Our ultimate goal then is to find God in scripture. The whole goal of the Bible is to discover and grow in a relationship with God through Jesus Christ. Any other purpose for scripture is misguided and dangerous.

Trying to explain this approach may at first seem much harder than it really is. But there are plenty of resources to help even a beginner begin to dig deeper into scripture to find the truths of God himself.

Think about it: Why is it that if we have God out of focus in our hearts and our minds, everything else in the world will be out of focus?

_____
_____
_____

Application: How will "getting God in focus" and into the proper perspective in your own life positively affect your whole life?

_____
_____
_____

In determining how to apply the truths of God in our personal and church lives, we must understand how truth comes from God. Our "theology" is our belief about who and what God is—his personhood and existence. Paul said that, "God's invisible qualities—his eternal power and divine nature—have been clearly seen, being understood from what has been made…" (Rom. 1:20). In other words, the creation itself shows us much about our

Creator God. The Bible then explains a lot of what we see. Our theology, formed from our study of creation and the Bible, is what we believe about God's character and purposes. Further, our doctrine flows from our theology. "Doctrine," for our purposes here, comprises our religious beliefs, application, and practices. Finally, our behaviors and lifestyles grow out of our theology and doctrine. God does what he does because of who he is. Ultimately so do we. Our beliefs about God determine our beliefs about ourselves, others, and the world around us. And in reality what we truly believe about God can better be seen in our ways of life than merely through our words. To become like him, we must also begin to do things according to who he is, not who we are apart from him. As we do what he does and otherwise asks us to do, his Spirit changes us to be like him inwardly and then outwardly (2 Cor. 3:18). Thus we do the things we do because they help us to be what we seek to be—like God.

In a troubling passage, Jesus said that at the final judgment, there would be many Christians who had been very religious and active as Christians but whom Jesus had never come to know (Matt. 7:21–23). Note particularly verse 22, "Many will say to me on that day, 'Lord, Lord, did we not prophesy in your name and in your name drive out demons and in your name perform many miracles?'" These will be those of us who have been doing things in the name of God and even claiming the power of his Holy Spirit but who Jesus says will find it all for naught because these will have never been in a saving relationship with him. Further, John said the test of our having come to know Jesus was if we were being obedient to him (1 John 2:3–6). This is consistent with many other clear statements the Bible makes. However, if doing the "Christian" things that Jesus spoke of—prophesying, driving out demons, and even performing miracles—are not necessarily signs that we are saved and are being obedient to God, what is? That's what this drawing tries to help us understand how to truly be obedient to God on the inside as well as on the outside.

Figure 4: Living Out the Truth of God

Christ and scripture reveal God to us first as a person and then in principles. These then help us determine how we are to live out these principles in daily life. In addition to what we do outwardly, God sees our thoughts and feelings as "behaviors" as well, and thus so much of what we are asked to do has more to do with how we "behave" inwardly than how we behave outwardly. Jesus said if we are to be clean on the outside, we must first be cleaned on the inside (Matt. 23:26).

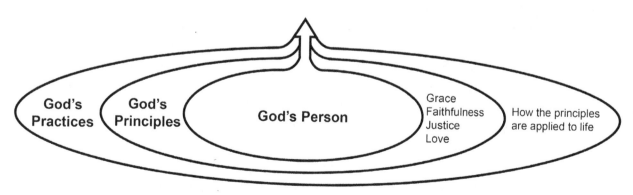

When we find the truth of God, we are ready to learn how to live as Jesus lived and planned for us to live. In Romans 1:18–25, Paul explains that when we "exchange the truth of God for a lie," our worship becomes about us and the world around us rather than about God. And if we miss God, we miss truth. Period.

Consider:
In the diagram above, four particular principles are revealed that describe God's personal nature. They are that he is graceful, faithful, loving, and just. What do each of these mean in modern English and in our present-day society?
_____
_____
_____

Why might it be very important to define these virtues or principles of God based on how God expressed them in his own person, rather than simply assuming the definitions of our modern language?
_____
_____
_____

How does the way God exhibits these virtues or principles differ from our modern understanding of them?
_____
_____
_____

Apply: How can you apply these and other godly virtues in your own life?
_____
_____
_____

So far in this lesson we have seen the Bible as a two-paned window through which we see God depicted in biblical history (fig. 1). We then considered the Bible as a lens by which we can first see and then truly discover Jesus and by doing so discover God (fig. 3). Lastly, we looked at how by working from the inside of God to the outside of ourselves, we can use our knowledge of God to propel and constrain what we believe, who we are, and how we live our lives in regard to that knowledge (fig. 4).

Figure 5 below is a very brief depiction of the history covered in the Bible. To the far left are the ages of Bible history, sometimes called "dispensations," with the contextual beginning and end of each given. The second column shows the various periods within each of these. Some key figures who lived during the various periods are listed in the third column. In the last column, a simple list of some of the empires that affected biblical history is given. None of these are exhaustive by any means but are given to help gain a simple overall view of Bible history that will allow us to better contextualize the various individuals, stories, and writings we encounter in scripture.

In modern terms, this would be like trying to understand a specific historical event from the perspective of the United States. Take, for example, if one were trying to understand the implications of an event, such as the Boston Tea Party. The age involved would be the history of the United States of America. The period involved would be the American Revolution. Key figures might be seen as Samuel Adams, John Adams, George Washington, and so forth. Key world empires involved would be England and perhaps France.

Consider:

Why would it be impossible to understand and interpret the implications of an event like the Boston Tea Party without understanding the greater historical picture or context surrounding it?

_____
_____
_____

Figure 5: Periods of Bible History

Ages	Periods	Key Figures	World Empires
	Creation		
PATRIARCHAL	Before the Flood	Adam and Eve	
	After the Flood	Noah	
	Patriarchs	Abraham	
	Egyptian Bondage		
	The Exodus	Moses	
	Giving of the Law		
MOSAIC	Wilderness Wanderings		
	Conquest of Canaan	Joshua	
	Judges	Sampson	
	United Kingdom	David	Assyrian
	Divided Kingdom		
	Kingdom of Judah		Babylonian
	Babylonian Captivity	Daniel	
	Restoration of the Jews		Medo-Persian
	Between the Testaments		Greek
	Life of Christ		
	Cross		
CHRISTIAN	Death and Resurrection		Roman
	Church	Apostles	
	Present		
	Judgment		

Note the three major Bible ages (sometimes called "dispensations") in the first column. Then notice in the second column the corresponding periods of Bible history within each of the ages. The third column lists a few key figures from each. The fourth column shows some of the important empires that impacted Israel and then the early church.

So in conclusion, this lesson has covered the Bible conceptually in several ways—as a window, as a lens, and as a way to determine from it how we are to act and live. We have considered the Bible's design—the books, the two Testaments, and the groupings within each. Lastly, we considered the overall historical times contexts of scripture. This lesson can serve as an important foundation to continue learning about the design of the Bible and thus allow it to be interpreted more accurately and effectively.

Self-Reflection

1. List some of the major ways you have previously viewed the Bible (e.g., as simply a "good book" and as devotional material.)?

2. How has my view of the Bible impacted my beliefs about God and other spiritual things, if in fact it has had such an effect?

3. How can understanding some basic aspects of the scripture design help me better read and understand the Bible?

4. How does seeing the Bible as a window through which I can see God differ from my perhaps seeing the Bible as God or thinking God was only active during Bible times?

5. In what ways might I have defined important godly virtues using a modern societal perspective rather than defining them by the personality of God himself as he has revealed himself through Christ and the Bible?

6. How has my modern definition of certain virtues perhaps negatively affected my views of God?

7. What, if any, Bible stories can I think of that teach about God's character? (Use the spheres in figures 3 and 4 to try to understand and apply.)

LESSON 2
Understanding the Inspiration of the Bible

INTRODUCTION

GOD SAID CENTURIES AGO, "THIS is the one I esteem: he who is humble and contrite in spirit, and trembles at my word" (Isa. 66:2). If you want to have a good relationship with God, you must have a deep respect for his Word. The purpose of this lesson is to tackle the challenge of understanding biblical inspiration. God's people, beginning with Israel and continuing with the church, have always had a tradition of very carefully writing, copying, translating, and preserving those writings that were deemed as inspired. As noted in Lesson 1, "Bible" is the title most give to the sacred writings handed down from Israel and the church. The Bible mostly calls itself the "scriptures" (John 5:39) or the "holy scriptures" (2 Tim. 3:15). The Old Testament writings are referred to as "The Law and the Prophets" (e.g., Matt. 5:17; 7:12; 22:40). Jesus once referred to it as, "the law of Moses, and in the prophets, and in the psalms" (Luke 24:44). Peter also refers to the writings of Paul as "scriptures" (2 Pet. 3:15–16).

However, the Bible does not generally refer to itself as "the Word of God" per se as many do today. In the scripture Jesus is called "the Word" (John 1:1). The Word of God is the essence and the truth of God as revealed in Jesus himself. But the scriptures clearly do refer to themselves as the words or writings *from* God. It might then be said that we come to know the Word *of* God (the truth of God) by the words *from* God (the scriptures). But the Bible is not God, and it must not be "worshiped" as a Christian idol.

The Old Testament and then the New Testament were collected and assimilated into the Bible over the centuries. What was being done by the scribes and editors was the important and serious work of identifying, collecting, and preserving the writings of those writers deemed by Israel and then the church to be prophets speaking from God. These were considered "inspired." The modern English word "inspired" has come to mean something less than "God-breathed," as it did when first used in English translations of the Bible, such as the King James Version. The Greek word used in the New Testament meant that the message came directly from God. The modern word "inspired" means one is spiritually or mentally aroused and imbued with a special ability to speak or write. Most do not mean that it is literally coming from God though.

Thus today any discussion of biblical inspiration must come with such an explanation about what is meant. Many see inspiration as meaning the scriptures were dictated spiritually by God and that the original writers were merely writing the exact words God was putting in their heads. This is where the modern views of infallibility (completely reliable) and inerrancy (without any errors or inaccuracies) come from. Others believe inspiration is concerning the core messages and meanings but not necessarily in the wording itself. Still others believe it was only from God in that the writers were good men of God who were writing from their own knowledge and experience of God. Of course many outside of Jewish and Christian circles do not believe the Bible is from God at all. Suffice it to say, the diversity in these views of the Bible causes tremendous controversy and division in the Christian church.

Consider then some concepts and scriptures concerning the God origin of scripture or biblical inspiration.

Key Scripture: Psalms 119:89, 152—As God is eternal, his Word is eternal because the Word is the essence of the truth of God.

1. In Psalms 119, God's Word is praised and honored repeatedly. Many believe King David wrote it. Others have suggested Ezra or Daniel. This beautiful psalm was referring at the time of its writing to the part of the scripture that had already been written and that was considered most sacred to the Jews, the Torah or the Law. Psalms 119 is the longest of the psalms, and it is as well the longest chapter in the entire Bible. It has one hundred seventy-six verses; more verses than fourteen of the Old Testament and seventeen of the New Testament books. Check out this chapter in your Bible. What might the mere length of this Psalm suggest about the importance of this topic?
   _____
   _____
   _____

2. Why is it significant to know that God's Word is eternal?
   _____
   _____

3. How might the knowledge that God's Word is eternal affect our view and approach to it?
   _____
   _____
   _____

Further Study

1. What does each of these scriptures have to say about God's Word?
   a. Isaiah 40:8
      _____
      _____
      _____

   b. Matthew 24:35
      _____
      _____
      _____

   c. 1 Peter 1:25
      _____
      _____
      _____

2. Correlate the message of those three verses with that of John 1:1, 14.

Key Scripture: John 1:1–14—Jesus is himself the Word of God.

1. Since Jesus is called the Word of God, it might be helpful to our understanding and application to refer to scriptures as words from God. How might that way of thinking about the Bible help us in finding and experiencing God?

2. The Gospel of John is one of the last books written in the New Testament, and some consider John as the official biographer of Jesus. Explain in your own words what John is saying in verses 1 and 14.

3. To find God in the Bible, why is it important to look for the Word of God within the words from God?

4. What could be the result of our reading of the scripture if we fail to see Jesus through it (John 5:39)?

5. How then would you explain the difference between Jesus as the Word of God and the Bible as the words from God?

Further Study

1. In Colossians 1:16, Paul says Jesus created all things. Hebrews 11:3 tells us that the world was framed by God's command (literally "God's Word"; see multiple translations). Further, Hebrews 1:3 tells us that everything in creation is sustained by God's powerful Word. What observations might be made in relating these three verses?

2. In John 5:39–40, why do you think the Jews failed to look for the Word of God (Jesus) in the words from God?

3. Pay specific attention to John 5:37–38. What result did failing to see Jesus have in their own personal lives?

Key Scripture: 2 Timothy 3:16–17—The early church recognized certain writings or scriptures, as "God-breathed" (inspired) and determined that these writings should be carefully used and followed.

1. What do you think it means that all scripture is "God-breathed"?

2. Since the whole New Testament had not even been written, let alone assembled, what scripture was Paul likely referring to at this point?

3. What does it mean that scripture "thoroughly equips" us?

4. According to this text, explain what the scripture is specifically designed for?

Further Study

1. In view of the prediction of Paul in 2 Timothy 4:2–4, why is a clear understanding of God's Word especially important for us today?

2. In Colossians 3:16, what does it mean to let the Word or "message" of Christ dwell richly among you?

3. What could easily happen in church communities where God's words are not carefully studied and applied?

Key Scripture: James 1:22–25—The scriptures are not just for devotional reading and personal comfort. They are to be obeyed and applied. Merely reading or listening to the Word but not obeying is a deceptive and a dangerous trap.

1. How is it that one can listen to the Word and not do what it says?

2. What motivations would cause us to not put what we learn into practice?

3. How can hearing but not obeying prove deceptive to others and ourselves?

4. How can we be assured we are following the Word of God in our obedience to the words from God as found in the scripture?

Further Study

1. Read Colossians 2:8. What kinds of things does Paul say might be most likely to lead us away from the pure, unadulterated Word of God?

2. How can we make sure that our interpretations of scripture align with our understanding of Christ, the Word of God?

3. In 2 Corinthians 11:3, Paul expresses fear that the Corinthians will be corrupted from a pure and sincere devotion to Christ. How can religion in general, and even Christianity specifically, possibly lead us away from a sincere devotion to Christ rather than to it?

Key Scripture: Matthew 7:13–23—Being "Christian" does not necessarily mean one is saved, or "known" by Jesus (i.e., in a safe relationship with him). The scriptures are what guide us to a right kind of relationship with him rather than allowing us to fall into a rote religion called by his name.

1. The word "life" used in this scripture means spiritual, eternal life—life as God experiences it. What does Jesus say about finding this life, and what does this mean?

2. What description does Jesus give of the false prophets?

3. Describe what a current-day false prophet might look like.

4. In verse 23, what do you think Jesus is saying about many of those who call on his name as their savior and Lord?

5. How can unsaved "Christians" do all the spiritual things Jesus says many will have done but still not be known by him (verses 22–23)?

6. How can knowing God through the scriptures keep us from being one of these deceived ones?

7. In what ways do you suppose individuals can feel they know Christ and yet Christ not know them?

Further Study

1. Read 1 John 2:3–6. What is the test of whether one truly knows God or not?

2. How can one be so deceived about something so important?

3. Relate verses 4 and 6. Note that obeying Jesus is the same as living as Jesus lived, rather than just doing religious things or obeying human concepts and teachings. Why do you think this is so?

4. In 2 Timothy 2:19, Paul says the Lord knows those who are his. Why is this important for each of us to realize this?

5. What is the difference in us knowing Jesus versus him knowing us?

6. In Galatians 4:9, Paul seems to reverse himself midsentence in this regard when he speaks of our knowing God and then says, or rather, you "are known by God." Given what we have seen so far, why might he take care to make this distinction?

7. In John 12:47–48, Jesus says it is his word that judges us. What do you think he means?

Key Scripture: Hebrews 4:12–13—God's Word is living and active! The words of scripture are not merely bits of information, but rather they have divine power behind them. They bring life to us because they have the life of God in them.

1. What descriptions are given here for God's Word?

2. What all does this scripture say God's Word does for us and to us?
   _____
   _____
   _____

3. What does it say the Word does for God?
   _____
   _____
   _____

4. How do you think words can have the power of God behind them and in them?
   _____
   _____
   _____

5. How should the truths of this text impact each of our view of and our study of both the Word of God (Jesus) and the words from God (scriptures)?
   _____
   _____
   _____
   _____

Further Study

1. In John 15:3, relate what does Jesus say his Word had done for the apostles? Relate that to what Hebrews 4:12-13 says the effects of God's Word are.
   _____
   _____
   _____

2. What does Paul call the Word of God in Ephesians 6:17, and what do you surmise that to mean?
   _____
   _____
   _____

3. Read and consider Proverbs 14:12. Why should this reality spur us to strive to understand the truth of God found in the scripture rather than to believe mere human interpretations of it that may simply be designed to pander to what we would like to believe the truth to be?
   _____
   _____
   _____

4. Read Colossians 2:8, and relate it to Proverbs 14:12.
   _____
   _____
   _____

5. Read and consider Jeremiah 17:9 and 1 Corinthians 4:4. Many claim to be "certain" of knowing God because of what is in their hearts, by how they feel, or that their consciences are clear. What is the danger of determining the validity of our relationships to God merely by how we feel?

6. How can we protect against being deceived by the feelings of our hearts?

Key Scripture: 2 Peter 1:3, 16–21—The Christian faith is not a blind faith any more than science, with its theories and hypotheses, is blind. As with many other fields of study, both should be based on reason and evidence. The evidences for the Christian faith can be disputed, just as scientific observations and conclusions can be disputed, but objective people can hardly deny the evidences and testimonies. As a point of evidence, the apostle Peter testifies in writing that he is an eyewitness of Jesus, particularly that God spoke from heaven saying Jesus was the Son of God. Thus Peter urges readers to pay attention to what has been said. He says that the reality of the divinity of Jesus validates the testimony of all the prophets that had come before.

1. According to verse 3, what does our knowledge of Christ do or provide for us?

2. As if on a witness stand giving his eyewitness account, what is Peter's testimony about Jesus?

3. According to Peter, in verse 19, what does the validity of Jesus as the Christ, the Son of God, do for the rest of the Bible and its prophecies?

4. What does Peter say that we must understand "above all"?

5. Why do you suppose this must be understood "above all" in order for us to find God through the scriptures?

6. Given its divine origin, what does Peter say our response to scripture ought to be?

Further Study

1. Read 1 Timothy 4:16. How does Paul's admonition to Timothy relate to Peter's admonition that we should pay attention to God's message (2 Pet. 1:19)?

2. What does Paul mean by "life" and "doctrine"? (It might be helpful in considering this to review figure 4 from Lesson 1.)

3. Given the gravity of this, how much effort should be given to considering God's will concerning our own lives and doctrine?

4. Why do you suppose so many, even among Christians, give so little time and effort to their study of God's Word?

5. How can we overcome this trap ourselves?

6. In 1 Thessalonians 2:13, Paul refers to their seeing his messages to them as the Word of God. How should seeing the Bible as God's words affect the way we view and respond to it?

Self-Reflection

1. How have I previously viewed biblical inspiration?

2. How has studying this lesson affected my views of it?

3. What questions do I have concerning biblical inspiration that I need to seek answers to or understanding about to move forward?

4. How can I improve my knowledge and understanding of the Bible?

5. What is my best takeaway from this lesson?

6. What is the one action I will take in regard to this lesson?

LESSON 3

The Story of the Bible

Introduction

Although the Bible is a collection of books written by various prophets through the ages, it has a tightly woven cord running through it. One of the greatest challenges of studying the Bible is coming to see and understand this story that winds its way through all the Bible books and through all of the history that it records, in order to bring us to Christ. From the creation to man's fall into sin; from God's work with and through Israel to bring about the Messiah to the establishment of the kingdom on earth to await Christ's final return and judgment, there is an interlocking story revealing God's eternal purpose. It is often called the scheme of redemption or the plan of salvation. The purpose of this study is to see where this cord from God leads—straight to Jesus—and to understand how it leads us there!

Trying to summarize this story into a single lesson is perhaps even more daunting than trying to understand the story itself. Broad sections of scripture are being all too briefly summarized here, thus running the risk of even misrepresenting them. So let the student beware in this study. This is an overview and not a detailed analysis by any stretch of the imagination. There are whole books written to try to summarize this story, and they can be helpful in a more extensive analysis. This lesson, however, is designed to be as brief as possible to help you gain a working, overall knowledge of this story so that later study and analysis can be accomplished more effectively.

Key Scripture: Genesis 1:1–2—There is a creator and designer of the universe. No two verses of any writing bear more heavily on an understanding of who we are as humans and what our purpose is for being here. These verses from the Bible's very beginning stake their claim against atheism by claiming that there is indeed a God who created the world. It stakes its claim against humanism by clearly asserting that the universe was made by God and for God (Col. 1:16). They stake their claim against what I call "scientism"—the "religion and faith" of much of science that believes the physical world is all there is and therefore all of life's answers are to ultimately be found in science. These verses make the clear claim that before there was matter there was God and that his is the ultimate energy that became the original matter of this universe of ours.

1. What does the Bible say about creation?
___
___
___

2. The Bible simply assumes God and never really seeks to prove he exists. Why do you suppose that is?

3. Read Psalms 14:1. Why do you think the Bible would assert that it is foolish to not believe in God?

4. Why might it make more sense to believe there is a creator to the universe than to believe that the universe somehow self-generated?

5. Why then might it take more of a leap of faith to NOT believe in God than it does TO believe in God?

6. Given the simplicity and brevity of the original statements about creation, how might these be easily misused?

Further Study

1. The creation story of Genesis 1 and 2 is written in a kind of poetic, expressive style using the kind of account and the language of creation that had already spread among the nations by the time Genesis was finally written. In that it is poetic, it is clearly symbolic in nature, as it is summarizing lengthy and complicated events and processes. Its aim is clearly to draw humankind back to its creator rather than to give a detailed scientific account of exactly what God did and even more so how he did it. Although the thought of Genesis not being completely literal, but rather symbolic, is galling and frightening to fundamentalism (this is a particular view and use of scripture that claims everything in the Bible is to be taken literally), the use of symbolism, various manners of speech, and different forms of literature do not mean it does not come from God or reveal truth. Rather the reader is expected to make interpretations and associations and to draw meaning from the descriptions and such. There has long been considerable debate over a variety of aspects of the creation story, such as the order of creation, whether the days are literal twenty-four-hour days, and how scientifically accurate are the other processes that are being described, to name a few. However, this creation account cannot simply be viewed from a scientific perspective for at least two reasons: the original authors knew nothing about our scientific method nor did they set out to establish a scientific account of the creation. Science can ultimately only discover what the truth is. At least that should be the goal (and to assume that all scientists and all of science is completely objective and without personal agendas is very naïve). Thus there will not in the

end be a disagreement between a correct assessment of the creation story and what science finds to be true. Of course science can never definitively describe how many things came about because they occurred eons ago and cannot be directly observed. Often lost in the debate is how amazing it is that ancient biblical writers were able to accurately describe what they did without the benefit of science. It is also amazing the tools science has found to study the universe both near and far as well as back to the world's origin. What do you suppose the most relevant principles from the Bible's creation account are?

2. In Romans 1:18–20, how does the Bible say that even one with little knowledge can see and know God?

3. In the same text, what does Paul mean in saying, "unbelieving people are without excuse"?

4. According to his statements in Matthew 7:7–8, what is Jesus's promise about where our honest seeking will lead us?

5. Read the story in Acts 8:26–33 of the Ethiopian who was seeking truth and was sent a prophet to teach him. Do you believe God can and will answer any truth seeker similarly?

6. In the same way, we read in Acts 10:1–48 about a man named Cornelius, a Roman, who was also seeking truth. God sent Peter to him. Why was it unusual that Peter, a Jew, was sent to this non-Jewish household?

7. The Old Testament prophet Jeremiah told the children of Israel who had been dispersed to countries far away from Israel that they would find God when their seeking became wholehearted (Jer. 29:13). How does wholeheartedly seeking God compare with, say, halfheartedly seeking him?

Key Scripture: Genesis 1:26–27—The whole creation declares God's power and his nature, but only man is made in God's very image. Science and anthropology both find that mankind has been extraordinarily

conscious, artistic, creative, ingenious, communal, and, yes, spiritual from humankind's earliest days. Humans are in fact spiritual beings like God.

1. There is significant debate about why the Bible renders God as saying, "Let us make man in our own image..." This first-person plural expression for God is found only four times in scripture (Gen. 1:26–27; 3:22; 11:7, and Isa. 6:8). The traditional Christian view is that this is a reference to God's triune or threefold nature as the Father, the Son, and the Holy Spirit (Matt. 28:19). Recently, however, other explanations seem to be dominating the discussion. Whatever its actual meaning and purpose is, this expression seems to clearly indicate that God, the "Majestic Glory," is not to be easily expressed in simple terms. In a sentence or two write out how you have previously seen and defined God.

   _____
   _____
   _____

2. What is the significance of our being created in God's image?

   _____
   _____

3. How would knowing more about God's nature help each of us?

   _____
   _____
   _____
   _____

Further Study

1. In John 4:23–24, how does Jesus describe God's nature?

   _____
   _____
   _____

2. How would you define what it means to be a spirit?

   _____
   _____
   _____

3. Summarize in your own words the meaning and implications of Genesis 1:26–27 in regard to our finding God through scripture.

   _____
   _____

4. The Bible calls the first humans "the man" and "the woman." The man's name was Adam, which simply meant "man." The woman's name was Eve, which means "living," because she would become the mother

of all the living (Gen. 3:20). If the expressions "the man" and "the woman" were to be used in the place of "Adam" or "Eve" in the text, how might that affect your view of the original humans?

_____

_____

5. What symbolism do you see as possible in the creation account and especially in the creation story of mankind?

_____

_____

6. In Genesis 2, we learn a bit about the Garden of Eden. It is not known for certain the precise location of the original Eden, although many feel surer than others. It is also not known for certain what "Eden" meant, although the original word might have meant "plain." Eden came to be referred to as paradise. We think in words, and therefore words are powerful in their effects on our beliefs and interpretations. For instance, if the text were to read, "Man and woman lived in the garden on the plain God had prepared for them," how might this more generic description affect your visualization of our human origins?

_____

_____

_____

Key Scripture: Genesis 3:1–7—**In the garden there were lots of trees, but two of them were key to the Bible story. There was also a tempter that comes as a snake. Mankind fails to trust God and disobeys him by eating from the "forbidden tree." This represents the choice of humans to turn to self-reliance rather than to rely on the grace and goodness of God. This incident describes the first or the original sin, which is often referred to as "the fall." The other key tree in the story is called the "Tree of Life." Mankind was free to eat from it and by doing so would possess eternal life. These two key trees in the garden represent the two paths we must choose from—self-reliance or God-reliance.**

1. The man and the woman were said to live in the perfect place and in a perfect union with God. The two trees that are key to the story—The Tree of Life and the Tree of the Knowledge of Good and Evil (Gen. 2:9)—are symbolic of the two choices mankind have in regard to a relationship with God. By their own admission, mankind was completely free to eat from all of the trees in the garden. How is the garden representative of the world we live in?

_____

_____

2. In Revelation 12:9, the apostle John tells us that the serpent is the devil (Satan) and that he leads the whole world astray. How did he deceive Eve and Adam?

_____

_____

3. What three temptations are identified in verse 6?

4. Consider 1 John 2:16, "For everything in the world—the lust of the flesh, the lust of the eyes, and the pride of life—comes not from the Father but from the world." How do these three worldly attributes relate to the temptation and how the couple looked at the forbidden fruit?

5. What do you think that the Tree of Life represents?

6. What does the Tree of the Knowledge of Good and Evil represent?

7. In what ways do we still live between the two options these two trees stand for?

8. How do you see that Satan may have deceived you or others close to you using the same sort of deceptions?

9. Why is this story called the Fall of Man, and why does it matter?

Further Study

1. In Romans 3:23, Paul writes that every human has sinned and fallen short of God's goodness. The New Testament word for "sin" is a Greek word (*hamartia*) that literally means "to miss the mark." How do you suppose "missing the mark" relates to "fall[ing] short of the glory of God"?

2. Why is each of us then under judgment against sin?

3. Clearly sin is contagious, spreading to all humans through all the ages (Rom. 5:12). In Psalms 51:5, David says he was sinful from birth. Christians have disagreed for centuries about the implications of the "original sin" in Eden and whether the punishment for sin is inherited from birth. Why did Paul say death spread to all men, and why do you think this might be important to the story of the Bible?

4. In Romans 5:1–2, Paul says that we are justified, or forgiven by God, because of our faith in God. If faith is required for salvation, what might the implication be of whether infants and children are under the curse of sin before they can respond in faith?

5. In Romans 6:23, what does Paul say is the curse for sin, and what is the free gift of God?

6. How does this relate back to the two trees in the garden and the implications of eating of either?

Key Scripture: Genesis 3:14–19—Because of the introduction of sin into the world, curses fall on humankind as well as on Satan.

1. The curse of sin God had promised as the consequence of eating from the forbidden tree in Genesis 2:17 ("you shall surely die") fell upon humankind because of their lack of trust in and obedience to God. The first curse, however, came to the devil himself. What do you think the curse placed on the serpent is all about?

2. The promise of Genesis 3:15 was that a man ("he") born from woman ("the seed of woman") would be the one that "crushed" the serpent's (Satan's) head. Not only has this widely been recognized as the first promise of Christ, the Savior of mankind, but it may also give indication that he would be born only of woman and not of man (this is not definitive, however, because of some of the wording). This will be repeated through the scripture as the "Seed" promise (Gal. 3:16). Although more recently this interpretation is also being seriously questioned by some, it still seems likely the original "seed of woman" promise

is the same one that is passed to Abraham, Isaac, and Jacob concerning God blessing the world through their offspring or seed (Gen. 12:7; 13:15; 24:7). How do you suppose this "seed of woman" is to ultimately crush Satan's head (Rom. 16:20)?

_____
_____
_____

3. The language in this text has a poetic quality to it, using symbolism to get the point across. What does "enmity" (hostility) symbolize that is to exist between Satan and the woman and between Satan's seed and her seed?

_____
_____
_____

4. How does Satan bruise the heel of Christ (Isa. 53:5)?

_____
_____
_____

5. What were the curses on woman?

_____
_____
_____

6. Why do you suppose these came about?

_____
_____
_____

7. What might these be symbolic of?

_____
_____
_____

8. What was the curse on man and what symbolism can you see in it?

_____
_____
_____

9. What is the curse on all humankind?

_____
_____
_____

10. The rest of the Bible reveals God's plan for delivering us from our sin curse while God carries out the curse on Satan! How have you felt the weight of the curse of sin in your own life?

_____
_____
_____

Further Study

1. Satan is called by numerous names. Consider for a moment a few of them and their meanings. How can understanding his names help us better understand his work against us?

   _____
   _____

   a. "Satan" means adversary and is used as his title fifty-three times (for instance, Job 1:6–9; Matt. 4:10).
   b. "Devil" comes from the Greek word *diabollos* meaning "slanderer or defamer" (Matt. 4:1, 5, 9; Eph. 4:27; Rev. 12:9; 20:20).
   c. Jesus calls him "Father of all Lies" (John 8:44).
   d. "Serpent" refers back to his original presentation in the Garden (Rev. 12:9; 20:2).
   e. "Prince of this world" indicates his rank and power in the world as it presently is (John 12:31).
   f. "Tempter" indicates his work in resisting God by luring men into sin (Matt. 4:3; 1 Thess. 3:5).
   g. "Accuser of the brethren" indicates his hateful role in demeaning and undermining God's people before God (Rev. 12:10).

2. How have you personally seen or experienced Satan in any of the ways these names describe him?

   _____
   _____

3. The Tree of the Knowledge of Good and Evil is symbolic of righteousness that is achieved by obeying the law. Since mankind is incapable of completely keeping any law of right and wrong, when that path was chosen, death was chosen. Thus death's curse came over all mankind. Paul said that Jesus could save because he had removed the curse of the law (Gal. 3:11). For those who respond to Christ by putting their faith in him alone, God has allowed them to eat again from the Tree of Life. Christ is the Tree of Life. It might be said that the world is the Garden, and the two key trees still exist in principle. How do you see that might be so?

   _____
   _____
   _____

Key Scripture: Genesis 4:1–8—Because of the sin curse, a break occurred in the relationship between God and humankind. As a result, humans would subsequently have to seek God out rather than simply be able to walk with him as a matter of course. Because of the first sin, humankind was forced to live outside of the garden. Next comes a story of sacrifices being offered to God by two of Adam and Eve's sons, Cain and Abel. The story sheds light on the development of religion and worship. It demonstrates how the humans would now have to seek God out in order to find him. It also sheds light on another reality—that God does not simply accept whatever we offer to him in worship and service.

1. Why do you suppose God rejects Cain's offering (look for hints that may exist in the story itself)?

   _____
   _____
   _____

2. Why do you suppose God does not accept all human worship?

3. What untruths about God make it easy for us to assume that he does or even should accept all that we might call worship?

4. What do you think was likely at the root of Cain's disobedience?

5. How can you apply this story to your own life?

Further Study

1. According to Jesus in John 4:23–24, what are the two key characteristics of the kind of worship God desires from us and that he accepts?

2. Describe each of these characteristics in your own words.

3. What three characteristics of acceptable worship are mentioned in Hebrews 12:28?

Key Scripture: Genesis 6:5—Sin is a most pervasive and ever-present problem in the world. It is contagious and it is progressive. There are no present cures, but only treatments. There are no vaccines against it; everyone "catches" it. There are no excuses for sin but only reasons—very bad reasons. Sin is no joke, as we sometimes like to make it, but rather is to be taken very seriously. It in fact is the gravest of all human concerns. All that ails humanity is of sin. A key to understanding the story of the Bible is to understand the corrupting nature of sin in the world.

1. Once sin takes root in our individual lives and in society itself, what is the result? It spreads like wildfire. Once sin entered through Adam and Eve, their son fell and soon the whole world followed. Do you think

Genesis 6:5 is to be taken literally—that every one of their thoughts was evil all the time. Or could this be a figure of speech called "hyperbole" (an obvious and intentional exaggeration to strongly emphasize a point)? Also explain why you believe it is or is not necessarily dishonest to speak in hyperbole?

2. What are some examples of how we commonly use hyperbole in our speech and how we all understand that it is not to be understood literally but that emphasis is being placed on how extreme something may be?

3. What do you think are the key lessons for us from this verse?

Further Study

1. In 1 Corinthians 15:33–34, Paul describes the contagious nature of bad character. How and why is sin, which in fact causes bad character, so contagious to us as human beings?

2. Why is it so hard to teach even children to do what is right and so difficult for them not to do wrong?

3. Note what Eve said God had commanded them concerning the bad tree—"You must not eat fruit from the tree that is in the middle of the garden, and you must not touch it, or you will die" (Gen. 3:3). What is the symbolism here involved in saying they were not even to "touch" the fruit, and how might such a prohibition indicate that sin is contagious?

Key Scripture: Genesis 12:1–3—After Creation, the Fall, the Flood, the reestablishment of mankind on earth, and the Tower of Babel incident, God sets his plan into action—the plan that will eventually, through the Seed of Woman, crush Satan's head and deliver humankind from the curse of sin.

1. What are the four promises God made to Abram?

2. What was God's purpose for Abram (later to be called Abraham)?

3. How are all people blessed through Abram?

4. Abram descended from Noah's son Shem. This is how the Jews came to be called the Semites (from Shemites). However, Abram's father was polytheistic and worshiped other gods (see Josh. 24:2). Why do you suppose Abram turned out as he did, becoming the Father of our Faith and being used by God in such a profound and universal way to bless humankind?

5. The rest of the Bible after Genesis 12 is connected to God's fulfillment of the four promises given to Abram—building Abram's ancestry into the nation Israel, giving them a land of their own (Canaan), bringing about the promised Savior who would offer salvation to all men, and blessing and being blessed by others. How can understanding these four promises and their fulfillments, as described in the Bible, help us understand the story of the Bible?

Further Study

1. The apostle Paul said that when we come to believe in Christ we become offspring of Abraham and heirs to all the promises of God (Gal. 3:29). All along God intended to build a universal, spiritual nation or kingdom, which was to be free from the confines of the Law, by using an isolated, earthly nation or kingdom, which was in fact bound by the Law. Speculate on why you think God might have chosen to bring about salvation in this way?

2. What other implications can you see in the commands and promises God gave Abram in Genesis 12:1–3?

Key Scripture: Acts 7:2–55—In this sermon Luke records for us in the New Testament, Stephen summarizes to Israel's leaders the plan of salvation, the story of redemption, leading to Jesus Christ's death and resurrection. Israel had waited for centuries for the promised Messiah. However, convincing them that Jesus was the Messiah was a daunting task. The Old Testament prophets had predicted the nation of Israel's rejection of him. The Gospel of Matthew is clearly written to establish that Jesus was the promised Messiah of Israel. The apostles, prophets, and teachers of the New Testament went to great pains to prove that none other than Jesus could fulfill what the Old Testament prophets had predicted about him as the Messiah or Christ (Acts 17:1–4; 18:28).

1. Stephen was a Jewish Christian who was appointed as a special servant for the church in Jerusalem and was a prophet of God as well (Acts 6). In a sermon that he preached to the highest body of Jewish rulers in his day, the Sanhedrin, which included the high priest, he explains the story of the Old Testament leading up to Christ. Take some time to read and meditate on the story he tells. It is rather long, but it summarizes quite well the Old Testament story leading to Jesus. After reading his sermon, consider why it is important to understand this story in order to understand the gospel of Christ?

2. Why is it significant that he begins with Abram?

3. Why do you suppose the Jews ultimately rejected the story of the Bible concerning the salvation of mankind through Christ?

Further Study—Consider the key points along the historical trail Stephen preaches about.

1. Acts 7:2–8
    a. Genesis 17:5—God made the promise to Abram. His name was changed to Abraham. What are the meanings of both "Abram" and "Abraham"? (Definitions are listed in the margin or footnotes of many Bibles.)

    b. Abraham settled in the Promised Land. Where was the Promised Land? (Locate it on a map; many Bibles have them in the back.)

    c. See how many different names or designations you can find that are used for this area?

d. Abraham had a son, Isaac, the "son of promise." What promise?

e. Genesis 32:27–28—Isaac had a son, Jacob, whose name was changed to Israel. What does "Israel" mean?

f. Jacob (Israel) had twelve sons, the twelve tribal heads. List their names.

2. Acts 7:9–16
   a. The other eleven brothers were jealous of Joseph and sold him into slavery in Egypt, but God rescued Joseph so that after being Potiphar's slave and then a prisoner in Pharaoh's dungeon, he became a ruler over Egypt, answering solely to the Pharaoh. What important life lessons does this story suggest for all of us still today?

   b. A worldwide famine struck and Israel (Jacob) sent his sons to Egypt for food. There they met Joseph, and the family, numbering seventy-five in all, were allowed to settle in Egypt. What lesson can be learned by each of us from this story?

3. Acts 7:17–19
   a. The population of the Israelites greatly increased, and under the fearful rule of a new Pharaoh, the Jews were enslaved and oppressed. Their babies were even killed. Why do you suppose God would allow this to happen, given they were chosen by him to carry out his universal plan of redemption?

   b. Israelites = Jews = Hebrews = People of God. Why is it important to have some idea of all the different names or designations that are used for the same things?

4. Acts 7:20–29
    a. Moses was delivered by God's providence through the craftiness of his mother. How can it be that when certain people do certain things it is said that God did it?

    b. Moses was reared by the Pharaoh's daughter and educated in Egyptian schools. How do you think this affected Moses, both in positive and negative ways?

    c. When Moses had become an adult, he killed an Egyptian while trying to defend an Israelite. Next he tried to mediate a fight between two Israelites. They revealed their knowledge of his killing of the Egyptian. Moses fled Egypt to preserve his own life. Given he was raised an Egyptian, why do you think he might have been defending Israelites?

5. Acts 7:30–38
    a. God called Moses to Egypt to deliver the Jews from slavery. How does this story demonstrate what is said in Isaiah 55:8–9 and Hebrews 1:1?

    b. Moses went back to Egypt. It was there that God showed himself to be the sovereign ruler of creation through a series of plagues on Egypt. These are recorded in Exodus 1–12. Consider taking the time now or at least later to read these gripping accounts of these encounters of the natural world with the supernatural one. Why do you think God might have done it all this way?

    c. Although Pharaoh gave Moses and the Israelites permission to leave Egypt, he then pursued Moses and Israel, but he and his army were destroyed in the Red Sea. Perhaps you could go back and read this account Exodus 13–14. What does the apostle Paul relate this incident to in 1 Corinthians 10:1–4?

    d. God gave Moses "living words," the Ten Commandments at Mt. Sinai. These constitute the basis of the Law of Moses, commonly just called the Law. Read the Ten Commandments in Exodus 20:1–17. What might have jumped out at you as you read them?

6. Acts 7:39–47
   a. Israel did not listen to God's Word given through Moses but rather turned back to the ways of Egypt and committed idolatry. Why is it that in our sinful human natures that we do this kind of a thing over and over?

   _____
   _____

   b. Read in Exodus 19:1–8 the agreement or covenant God made with Israel. What did Israel agree to do in this covenant (verse 8)?

   _____
   _____
   _____

   c. As he promised (Deut. 28:49–57), God later allowed Israel to go again into the captivity of another hostile nation because of their repeated disobedience. What was the purpose of this?

   _____
   _____
   _____

   d. Read Deuteronomy 28 and ponder the blessings God promised if they would obey the laws of the covenant and as well the curses if they disobeyed, including being taken captive again by a foreign nation. What does the New Testament say was the ultimate result of their repeatedly breaking their covenant with God (Heb. 8:3–13)?

   _____
   _____
   _____

   e. What does Hebrews 8:10–12 say the New Covenant that was to come would be like?

   _____
   _____
   _____

   f. Moses then built the tabernacle, the mobile temple, and Solomon built the permanent temple later on; each the symbol of God's presence in Israel. The word "tabernacle" is a rarely used English word that simply means a place of worship. Why do you suppose God gave them a specific place of worship, given we can now worship God anywhere we are?

   _____
   _____
   _____

7. Acts 7:48–55
   a. The Jews missed the symbolism of the tabernacle in the wilderness and later the temple built in Jerusalem as God's presence among them, and they thought God in actuality only dwelled with their

nation. The whole universe is God's dwelling, as their own scripture affirmed to them (Jer. 23:24). What in our sinful human nature makes us as individuals and as groups of people think we can somehow gain a monopoly on God's presence?

___

b. What does Hebrews 8:5 say the tabernacle Moses built was an early copy of?

___

c. The Israelites became "stiff-necked" and self-righteous. Because they trusted in their ancestry and in their own ability to be "right," they resisted God's Spirit in their lives. How can a relationship with God, that is supposed to make us humbled and surrendered, ultimately become a source of evil pride and arrogance?

___

d. Jesus was and is the fulfillment of all God's plan in creation. In your own words, how does the Old Testament story, as outlined by Stephen, lead us to the conclusion that Jesus is indeed Christ, our Lord?

___

e. Jesus was killed because men want to be self-focused rather than God focused. How does this then hearken us back to the story of the two trees?

___

SELF-REFLECTION

1. How much of the overall Bible story did I previously know?

___

2. How might my lack of knowledge have hindered my knowing Christ well or at all?

___

3. How can understanding God's plan of salvation, which God instituted from the very beginning, help me in building or growing my faith and effectively relating to Jesus?
   _____
   _____
   _____

4. Which part of the Bible story amazes me the most and how can that amazement drive me forward in my walk with God?
   _____
   _____
   _____

5. What questions do I have that arise from this study?
   _____
   _____
   _____

6. What follow-up action will I take after studying this lesson?
   _____
   _____
   _____

LESSON 4
The Problem of Sin

INTRODUCTION

Sin is not a very popular subject. Yet sin is the bad news that makes the gospel of Jesus such good news. The more we discover the problem of sin in our lives, the more we are truly ready and eager to discover Jesus!

Sin is simply acting out our failure to trust God and live for the purposes for which he created us. The sin depicted in the Garden of Eden—the one committed by Adam and Eve—was the desire to be like, or equal with, God by knowing good and evil. In acquiring this knowledge on their own, they would not need to trust in God, or so they thought. With evil intent, they believed the deceiver's consummate lie—that they could be self-reliant, doing as they pleased and not answering to or depending on God.

Although plenty has been written about the topic of sin, this lesson is designed to define sin, to help us understand why it is such a problem, and to point out some key scriptures about sin. In addition, this lesson will explore some of the common things God calls sin while considering the nature of God that makes sin what it is. A solid trust in God requires a clear understanding of the devastating effects of sin both in the present, the future, and eternally. A clearer understanding of sin will also help us better grasp the merciful heart of God that leads him to freely forgive us through Christ. This is a particularly long lesson and it is not intended for you to complete it quickly or in a single sitting. Part 1 of the lesson deals with understanding sin better. Part 2 deals with recognizing sin and its awful consequences.

PART 1: UNDERSTANDING SIN

Key Question: Where did sin originate?

1. The story of the Garden of Eden in Genesis 2 and 3 gives a sweeping, poetic depiction of the first people.
    a. If you have not already done so, make the time to read these two chapters, as they lay the foundation of the Bible's revelations about sin.
    b. What are your immediate thoughts and insights after reading it?
    _____
    _____
    _____

c. How might your previous and perhaps even naïve, recollections of this story be altered by reading it?
___
___
___

2. Read Genesis 3:1–7, as it introduces us to humankind's fall into sin.
   a. This passage presents the reader with a very brief description of a much deeper and more complicated reality of sin and its origins, as well as the natures of humankind, Satan, and God. What are the key points of this story?
   ___
   ___
   ___

   b. To help understand some of the deeper principles involved with sin, consider briefly the book of Job, contained in the Old Testament books of poetry. This book is the story of a man named Job whom God allowed to be tested by Satan by being stricken with loss, destruction, and disease. You can look up a brief introduction and overview of this book if you would like a better description and understanding.
      i. In the story, Job tries to understand why God, in Job's way of thinking, caused or allowed such tragedies to come upon him. Three of his friends repeatedly gave him bad input and advice. Have you experiences that you can think of that might be similar?
      ___
      ___
      ___

      ii. After Job repeatedly questions God about all his personal misfortune, the Bible tells us God rebukes him in no uncertain terms, saying that Job (representing mankind in general) was incapable of truly understanding God's deeper purposes (Job 38–41). How can hardship and testing either weaken and destroy our faith in God or strengthen and build up our faith in God?
      ___
      ___
      ___

      iii. The many attempts at concrete explanations of God's purposes, as well as the "spiritualized" explanations, seem to fall painfully short of reconciling all that we see in scripture with all that we see in ourselves as humans within this universe around us. How have the doubts and questions you may have in this regard affected your own faith?
      ___
      ___
      ___

      iv. To many of us, perhaps science, philosophy, and anthropology seem to fall even shorter of explaining God, as their greatest minds plunge into the deep waters of meaning, purpose, and the divine. How has your secular learning impacted your own faith?
      ___
      ___
      ___

v. Trying to explain everything about God, everything about Satan and the origin of evil, and all about God's purposes and intentions in this creation is simply impossible. Why does this matter?

vi. The endeavor can in fact become downright dangerous, causing the kinds of speculations depicted by Job's perhaps well-intentioned but highly misguided friends. God was clearly not happy with them (Job 42:7). How can our close friends and family inadvertently hurt us spiritually during our own trials?

vii. One would need to read the book of Job to understand the full point being made in the story, but for the purposes of this study this succinct principle should suffice: reducing the character of God to a few simple ideas or principles is dangerous. How might the simplistic, childlike views that we have grown up with prove detrimental to growing a mature faith that deals effectively with this sinful world's cold realities?

3. Presumptive, speculative, and naïve thinking is likely one of the clear and present dangers of what is called The Tree of the Knowledge of Good and Evil, as found in the Garden of Eden. Note some of the following details from the garden:
    a. Humankind, both male and female, was made in the image of God (Gen. 1:26–27). What is God's image and nature (John 4:23–24)?

    b. God made humankind and breathed life into them. This was not just our life in the flesh, as all animals had; it was a spirit life as well. Man had a soul (Gen. 2:7). Man is depicted as coming from the ground, whereas woman is depicted as coming from man. God himself, however, created both of them. Why is it critical to the story to see that God was the designer and creator no matter how matter came to be arranged and creatures came to be?

c. There was a special place in the world designed by God where man and woman were given to live and it was called the " Garden of Eden" or a garden of delights. How might the Garden of Eden be symbolic of our world as a whole?

___

d. Humankind could eat freely from all the trees in the garden except for one of two "special" trees that are identified. Paul says that where God's Spirit is, there is freedom (2 Cor. 3:17). How does the garden then symbolize this freedom?

___

e. The Tree of Life and the Tree of the Knowledge of Good and Evil were in the middle of the Garden of Eden. The latter tree was the tree with the "forbidden fruit" (Gen. 2:8–9). What does this forbidden tree represent in this beautiful world that God has made?

___

f. By Eve's own explanation (Gen. 3:2–3), Adam and Eve had been told that they could eat from all the trees in the garden except for the Tree of the Knowledge of Good and Evil and that touching or eating fruit from that tree would bring death. Why was touching sin, even if they did not take a bite, already sinful, and how does this relate to our own "touching" of sin through impurity, lust, covetousness, etc.?

___

g. In the story, evil comes into the picture in the form of a serpent that is later identified as Satan himself. He tempts the humans first by telling them that if they ate the forbidden fruit that they would not die. Secondly, he tells them that in fact when they ate of it they would become like God, knowing good and evil in their own rights. What is the ultimate lie in all of this?

___

h. They try the forbidden fruit. This is the original sin and is called the "Fall of Man." Why might it be important to know the profile of the story of how sin entered our world?

___

4. The Bible then quickly reveals the devastating nature of sin on humankind.
   a. The curse of sin on man, woman, and on evil itself are pronounced (Gen. 3:14–19). What were these curses on Satan, woman, man, and humankind?

___

b. The first people are removed from the Garden and doomed to live "East of Eden" (Gen. 3:21–24). What does their removal demonstrate in the greater picture of humanity's relationship with God?

c. Worship is depicted in the sons of Adam and Eve, Cain and Abel (Gen. 4:1–16). Cain's offering is rejected; Abel's offering is accepted. In jealousy Cain kills Abel, and as a result, is "marked" in some way so as not to be harmed by others and is driven away from his family to become a restless wanderer. Why is it not surprising that the first recorded murder is over worship or religion?

d. What attitude was at the root of Cain's sin?

e. God is grieved that he had made humankind and determines to start over with a new bloodline from a man named Noah (Gen. 6:1–8). God causes a devastating worldwide flood. Eight people and a bunch of pairs of animals are preserved in order to repopulate the earth. What does Peter say the flood was symbolic of in 1 Peter 3:20–21?

f. Right after the flood, however, the world quickly became worse again. Though it did not completely revert back to the state of things as described in Genesis 6:5, and the world has never gotten much better since. What is the overall lesson to be learned from this?

5. The information we are given of early man is scant, and thus there has been much speculation about the topic. Seemingly countless questions are obvious to consider and can sometimes be troubling for anyone who is prone to overly analytical thinking. A few sample questions are shared below. Bible teachers and scholars have suggested lots of speculative answers to such questions over the years, but in reality these are unanswerable questions, because we are simply not given the information. However, trying to overly literalize these stories is wrought with peril. These questions are given to stimulate open-mindedness in thought, not to create doubt. Because we cannot answer a question, it does not mean there is no answer. But disciples are learners; learners are thinkers; and therefore all thinking must not be seen as dangerous.

   a. Since God is all knowing (omniscient), how could he have been so wrong about humankind and be portrayed as if he is surprised by our outcome?

b. Are the Garden of Eden, Adam and Eve, and the Two Trees to be taken completely literally or could they be figurative of a much greater depiction of the world?

c. Is the snake, or serpent, who tempted Eve and Adam figurative or was Satan actually posing as some kind of snake?

d. Did the snake actually talk to Eve, and she actually converse with it, and if so, how do you think this conversation might have actually looked?

e. Who did Cain and Seth marry, and where did these women come from, since there is no mention of others in the garden?

f. Were there possibly other children born in the Garden of Eden, and if not, why not? They had already been commanded to multiply while still in the garden (Gen. 1:28).

g. When Cain was cursed and sent out as a wanderer, who were the people that he was afraid would kill him, and where did they originate?

6. Following are some suggested working explanations of the Garden of Eden. By "working explanations" it is meant that these are not necessarily final answers, but they can be used to get the main points and move on to the bigger picture, as well as reconcile the account to many of the other realities not mentioned. Absolute literalists view this as liberal and not believing the Bible, but I believe it is an even more faithful attempt to understand the message of God here.

   a. The Tree of the Knowledge of Good and Evil and the Tree of Life represent humankind's free will to choose, or to not choose, to trust God—to let God be God instead of trying to be gods ourselves. These two options represent the two roads that Jesus depicts in the Sermon on the Mount in Matthew 7:13–14. One is the way to destruction, which is broad and easily traversed, and is the choice of the majority. The other is the way to life, which is narrow, not easy to stay on, and is the choice of only a few. The choice between the two roads represents the battle for a sense of control, which is waged by a child from the time she/he is born, and by all of us as humans as we encounter the world around us. At least this is the case until we surrender to God by an act of God's grace and of our God-given free will.

b. The Tree of Life ultimately represents Jesus himself, the underlying source of life for the whole universe (Col. 1:15–17). Jesus says that he is "the life" (John 14:6).
c. The Tree of the Knowledge of Good and Evil manifests itself in humanity's attempts to live by human reasoning—the "basic principles of the world." This knowledge itself is not all bad, but rather can be "holy and good," as with the Law itself. The problem with it is that humans are not designed to live by it. Knowing its realities simply puts us under the curse of guilt and condemnation. Its principle is manifested in the Law of Moses, and the Jews found it impossible to fully obey. It is also manifested in any spirit of legalism, humanly originated and designed to achieve some model of rightness that allows us to think we can be righteous by being right. Legalism is, however, totally destructive to human spirituality (Gal. 3:10).
d. The rest of the trees in the garden, all of which are delightful, represent human freedom of thought and experience in the universe.
e. The Garden of Eden represents our world of delights. As humans we have a seemingly endless capacity to be delighted through our minds, hearts, senses, and experiences. And there are countless opportunities all around us to utilize this capacity. The wrong choices, however, prove painful and destructive.
f. Unlike humans, all the other animals live by their basic instinct, driven, as we know now, from their lower brain.
g. Humankind was given the ability to choose to thoughtfully follow or not to follow basic desires and instincts. This higher part of our brains is often called the "executive brain," because through its capacity we can make choices that defy our basic fleshly instincts. Our soul and spirit must in some way connect to this part of our brains.
h. The serpent in the story represents Satan, the champion of evil, who for evil purposes tempts humankind to make choices that are counter to individual and social well-being.
i. The "Fall" into sin and the subsequent shame that follows seems to represent the "coming of age" found in adolescence, where nakedness and sexuality become sources of great embarrassment, often shame, and constant desires and temptations. Sin becomes a conscious, destructive reality during this time. Each individual, at that stage in her or his life, must deliberately choose the Tree of Life, which has been made available to us in Christ, or suffer a separation from God. This separation is represented in the story by their foolishness in attempting to hide from an omnipresent, omniscient God by standing in some bushes and covering their genitals with leaves!

7. Adam—the one man—represents humankind in general, who in his attempt to control his own destiny fails to trust the creator, and thus falls into the trap of destruction (Rom. 5:12-21). Jesus Christ, "the other man," represents Jesus who embodies God's redeeming plan of eternal life to those that choose him (Rom 5:18–19).
8. Sin in this world thus originated early in the birth and establishment of humanity, and its destructive effects are pervasive and ever-present among us all.
9. Humankind has not and cannot contrive its own remedy. In fact, human attempts to stem the tide of sin on its own are generally, and ultimately, more destructive than the sin itself!
10. In your own words, what are the key lessons taught from the sin story in the Garden of Eden?
_____
_____
_____

Key Question: What is sin?

1. Sin is at its core a failure to trust God's will, knowledge, wisdom, and guidance. It is rebellion. It is defiance. From reviewing the first sin in the garden, how do you personally experience and observe this tendency in your own life?
   _____
   _____

2. Sin is at its core an illegitimate and ultimately destructive way to find delight in the world around us. How do you see this in your own tastes of forbidden pleasures?
   _____
   _____

3. Sin is something that comes from inside of us, not something that comes from the outside. Reading Mark 7:20–23, what does Jesus say defiles us and what does it mean that it comes from inside of us?
   _____
   _____

4. In 1 John 3:4, in your own words, what does John say sin is?
   _____
   _____

5. In James 4:17, in your own words, how does James define sin?
   _____
   _____

6. In Romans 14:23, what does Paul say about sin, and what does this mean?
   _____
   _____

7. In summary of these last scriptures:
   a. Sin can be a violation of God's commands by something we do wrong.
   b. Sin can be a violation of God's commands by not doing something we ought to do.
   c. Sin can also be anything we do that is not acting out of faith in God or that is against our own beliefs about what is right and wrong.
   d. All of these are at the core a failure to trust God and respect who he is, what he is, and how he loves and wants the best for us.

8. The Greek word most often used in the New Testament for sin is *hamartia*, which literally means "missing the mark." The goal or mark we are to shoot for is nothing less than the glory and perfection of God (Matt. 5:48), and to sin even once means we have once and for all completely missed that mark! The

apostle Paul said we miss the mark by falling short of it, as when an arrow is shot at a target but hits the ground in front of it (Rom. 3:23). Think of an example of a particular sin you might be familiar with and consider how it is "missing the mark" of God's perfection.

_____
_____
_____

Key Question: How can we understand sin more fully by better understanding God's nature?

1. Since we are like him—as we are called his image bearers—God wants us to imitate him. Peter quotes God saying, "Therefore, with minds that are alert and fully sober, set your hope on the grace to be brought to you when Jesus Christ is revealed at his coming. As obedient children, do not conform to the evil desires you had when you lived in ignorance. But just as he who called you is holy, so be holy in all you do; for it is written: 'Be holy, because I am holy'" (1 Pet. 1:13–16; Lev. 11:44–45; 19:2). How have you previously thought about or defined the word "holy"?

   _____
   _____

   a. Look up the biblical definition of the word "holy."
   b. How and why does the word "holy" often carry a negative connotation?

   _____
   _____
   _____

   c. Is complete holiness something you think most people, even Christians, earnestly want and seek? Why or why not?

   _____
   _____
   _____

2. Some things to consider about evil:
   a. Evil is not the opposite of good, and Satan is not simply the evil counterpart of God.
   b. God has no equal (Psa. 40:5).
   c. Sin is a corruption of good, and Satan is a powerful, created angel that became the evil spirit that leads the present rebellion against God (Col. 1:16).
   d. Humankind bears the very image of God (Gen. 1:26–27).
   e. The universe was created by God and for his purposes (Col. 1:16–18).
   f. God, from the beginning, deemed the whole creation as good (Gen. 1:4, 9, 12, 18, 20, 25, 31), and that has never changed.
   g. This "good" world God made has, however, come under a curse and thus is corrupted. It is as oxidation corrupts iron causing rust to form and ultimately destroying layers of the metal itself. As Christ redeems each believer, one day the whole creation itself will be redeemed (Rom. 8:18–21). The rust will finally be removed to reveal the original creation.

h. In what ways do you see the forces of evil being portrayed as equal to or even greater than the forces of good in the world?

i. Why do you believe Satan wants himself seen as God's equal, and evil seen as the opposite of good rather than the corruption of good?

3. Read Ephesians 5:1–2 and John 4:23–24. Since we are image bearers of God, we are commanded to be imitators of him as beloved children imitate dearly loved parents. What do you think it means for a finite human to imitate an infinite God, who is a spirit (Note: this is a particularly hard question for some people, but it is one designed to provoke more open thought)?

4. Although the list could go on and on, consider these characteristics of God and the acts and attitudes that go against them and corrupt them in the world around us.
    j. God is holy, 1 Peter 1:15–16. To be "holy" literally means to be separate or set apart. That God is holy means that he is completely uncorrupted by the sin that presently exists in his creation. We are meant to be holy, but sin corrupts our holiness and draws us into worldliness. How does evil and sin corrupt our own holiness?

    k. God is love, 1 John 4:8. The word for the love of God is *agape* (Greek). It is the highest form of love. It is not a love of sentiment or feeling, but a love of the will that is based on truth and what is right. God wills what is best for his creation in general and for each individual in particular. How does sin corrupt this kind of love?

    l. God is good, Psalms 136:1. God always does what is best. Even the evil in the world will be worked out for the good (Rom. 8:28). How does evil corrupt good?

    m. God is meek and lowly, Matthew 11:29. The common human depiction of God, albeit more inferential than intentional, is as "high and mighty." This is however not how Jesus portrays God at all, and

Jesus is in fact "the exact representation of God" in the world (Heb. 1:3). Jesus revealed God as meek (gentle; humble) and lowly. God is most certainly all-powerful, and he is depicted as above all things. He is Lord and King! However, because of his nature, he leads as a humble, kind, generous, serving God (John 13:2–5; Phil. 2:5–8). How does evil corrupt God's design for us to be meek and lowly?

_____
_____

n. God is graceful, Ephesians 1:3–10. The word translated as "grace" is *charis* (Greek). It literally means gift. Our God is a giving God. His gifts are not to be earned or deserved. Something earned is by definition not a gift. Gifts can only be given. How does evil corrupt the very nature of giving, which is, giving expecting nothing in return?

_____
_____

o. God is compassionate, Psalms 103:8. The words translated as compassion in scripture generally mean, to have mercy, to feel sympathy, and to have pity on. Sadly, sympathy has even come to be seen in a negative light by many, as in, "I don't want your sympathy." How does evil corrupt the principle of compassion and sympathy in the world?

_____
_____

p. God is purposeful, Proverb 19:21. God has a purpose and that purpose is good, contrary to how this purpose is corrupted in the world. The world is often purposeless, beyond its hot pursuit of mere short-term pleasures. God's purpose means there is a good end in mind for what is done or what happens. Often this is not the case in the corrupted world. How does evil corrupt the goodness in purposefulness?

_____
_____

q. God is true, Romans 3:4. God is in fact truth itself (John 14:6). There is no lie or deceit in him. Satan however is a liar and the father of lies (John 8:44). How has evil corrupted truthfulness in the world?

_____
_____

r. God is faithful, Deuteronomy 7:9. God is completely reliable concerning his Word and promises (2 Pet. 3:9). He is completely trustworthy. He wants us to be trustworthy as well. How has faithfulness been corrupted by evil?

_____
_____

s. God is light, 1 John 1:5. The creation reflects the divine nature of God (Rom. 1:20). Light, as we see it in creation, is clearly a material manifestation of this special attribute of God. Light shows us the way. Light provides openness, honesty, and truth. Light shows us what is real. Light provides energy. Light represents security and hope. Although there are positive things to physical darkness within this creation, it often represents evil itself. How is spiritual darkness a corruption of the beautiful light of God?

Key Question: Why is Sin Such a Problem?

1. In Isaiah 59:1–2, what does God say our sin does regarding our relationships with him?
    a. What does this mean practically?

    b. Why is any kind of "separation" from God very serious?

    c. In Genesis 3, when Adam and Eve sinned, they were banned from the Garden of Eden, representing the separation sin brings between humankind and God. However, God still was in communication with them even when they were outside the garden. How can we be "separated" from God and still be in some kind of communication with him?

    d. In Genesis 4:1–16, after Cain had murdered his brother Abel, he was punished and banished even further than humankind had already been. The scripture says, "So Cain went out from the Lord's presence." Since he was alive and still living on earth, and God is present everywhere, in what way do you think that he was out of the Lord's presence?

2. In Romans 6:23, what does Paul say the penalty for sin is and what do you think this means?

a. Some have observed that the Bible seems to represents sin at two levels—at the macro level, meaning the overall concept of sin or sin in general, and at the micro level, meaning specific types and instances of sins.
b. Specific types of sins (e.g., greed and hatred) and instances of sin (e.g., a specific act of hatefulness) are merely an outgrowth and expression of sin in general. Thus where there is the presence of a single instance of sin, there is the presence of sin in general. Because sin brings death, every instance of sin is worthy of the penalty of death, since underlying each instance is the reality of sin within us.
c. Death is the loss of life. The Bible depicts death in two ways—death of the physical body and death of the human spirit due to separation from God. Sin brings both. Why do you think these two deaths might be connected?

_____
_____
_____

3. Read 1 Peter 2:11. What does Peter say our sinful desires do to us, and how do you see this in yourself and others?

_____
_____
_____

4. Read 1 Corinthians 6:9–10. What does Paul say will be the outcome of those who intentionally live in ways that are considered wicked by God?

_____
_____
_____

5. Read Revelation 21:8. How does Jesus depict the fate of those who continue to live in intentional sin?

_____
_____
_____

Part 2: Recognizing Sins and Their Awful Consequences

Key Question: What are some specific things God considers as sin?

1. There are a number of places in the Bible where various kinds of sins are listed.
    a. Read Exodus 20:1–17. This passage is the first recording of the Ten Commandments that God gave to Moses on Mount Sinai. These commandments form the basis of the Law of Moses, which includes over six hundred more laws, rules, and ordinances. Paul cites the violation of each of them as sin. He says the law is what makes sin known to us (Rom. 7:7). Briefly list the ten commandments in terms of what is the underlying sin of each that violates God's will for us:
        i. _____
        ii. _____
        iii. _____
        iv. _____
        v. _____

vi. _____
vii. _____
viii. _____
ix. _____
x. _____

b. In Matthew 22:35–39, Jesus summarizes the whole Law and Prophets in Two Great Commandments about loving God (the first four of the Ten Commandments) and loving others (the last six of the Ten Commandments). Any violation of one of the Ten Commandments is a violation of these two "love" commands.

c. Read the following verses from Jesus's Sermon on the Mount, and note how Jesus explained in greater depth some of the sins from the Ten Commandments and challenged the Jewish traditions surrounding them. List what the Jews had traditionally been taught and how Jesus amended an understanding of each.

i. Matthew 5:21
_____
_____
_____

ii. Matthew 5:27
_____
_____
_____

iii. Matthew 5:31–32
_____
_____
_____

iv. Matthew 5:33–34
_____
_____
_____

v. Matthew 5:38–39
_____
_____
_____

vi. Matthew 5:43–44
_____
_____
_____

d. Read Proverbs 6:16–19. List and briefly define for yourself the seven things this proverb says the Lord hates.

i. _____
ii. _____
iii. _____
iv. _____

v. _____
vi. _____
vii. _____

e. Read Galatians 5:19–21, listing and briefly defining each of the sins that Paul calls "works of the sinful nature."
   i. _____
   ii. _____
   iii. _____
   iv. _____
   v. _____
   vi. _____
   vii. _____
   viii. _____
   ix. _____
   x. _____
   xi. _____
   xii. _____
   xiii. _____
   xiv. _____
   xv. _____
   xvi. _____

f. After reading 1 Corinthians 6:9–11, list and briefly define each sin.
   i. _____
   ii. _____
   iii. _____
   iv. _____
   v. _____
   vi. _____
   vii. _____
   viii. _____
   ix. _____
   x. _____

g. Read Revelation 21:8. List and briefly define each sin.
   i. _____
   ii. _____
   iii. _____
   iv. _____
   v. _____
   vi. _____
   vii. _____
   viii. _____

2. These lists are by no means all-inclusive of the various things that can be identified as specific sins, however, together they give a more comprehensive list of specific and serious sins. What general observations might you make after looking over all of these lists?

___

3. Go back over the various sin lists and put check marks by the ones that are common in our world. Go back over a second time and put x's by the ones you believe to be common even among modern Christians. What thoughts do you have in doing this?

___

4. Special question #1: Is all sin somehow equal in severity? Although many wrongly conclude this, it may still be argued that all sin is somehow "equal." For instance, the idea is sometimes asserted that murder is really no worse than a "polite" or "white" lie. This view is based on the idea that all sin is harmful and destructive, and that for those not in Christ every sin carries with it a spiritual death penalty. However, far back in church tradition sins were recognized as "mortal" (most serious) and "venial" (less serious). And lists like the one above in Proverbs 6, demonstrate that to God there are more detestable sins than others. The above lists can thus help us be keen on some of the more destructive ones. Again, that is not to say that all sin is not serious, but to say we need to be careful about those among us who might try to justify some of the most destructive sins by saying they are no worse than other more unintentional or incidental sins with much less destructive power. Can you think of some instances where you or others might have tried to justify a very serious sin by thinking it is no worse than another less serious one?

___

5. Question #2: Can sins be categorized as a way of thinking about them. Although the scriptures do not specifically categorize sins this way, there are different types of sins. Consider the sin lists above along with other specific sins not listed. List a few sins under the following categories.
   a. What sins go against the human moral and spiritual natures, for instance, hatred?

   ___

   b. What sins go against our physical natures, for instance, sexual immorality?

   ___

   c. What sins go against God's plans and designs for us, for instance, making idols or failing to obey a specific command such as God commanding Moses to build a tabernacle?

   ___

Key Question: What are sin's effects and consequences?

1. Simply put, sin is harmful and destructive for very real reasons, even if we cannot at times figure out what is harmful about it. We humans must admit that we are limited in what we know. Of course we can never know what it might be that we do not already know! Under each of the following examples see if you can think of additional modern-day examples that may be similar.
    a. Physical or spiritual things in the history of humankind that were not at the time considered harmful but were later discovered to be quite detrimental, such as the use of certain drugs, tobacco use, forced slavery, polygamy, elitism, and sexism.

    b. Things that were actually considered socially beneficial but were later found out to be harmful—for instance, male domination, racial domination, caste system, prostitution, certain kinds of sexual abuse, human tyranny, and ungodly, self-serving monarchies.

    c. Things that as young people we did not consider harmful, but as we grew up we hopefully came to see differently, such as sexual impurity, pornography use, sexual immorality, petty fights, cliquishness, envy and jealousy, cheating in school, admiration of certain evil people, and rude behavior.

    d. Things as adults that we personally thought to be neither necessarily good nor bad and then later through spiritual development found out the opposite to be true, such as, premarital sex, abortion, cheating on taxes, unnecessarily violating laws we considered undesirable or unjust, and rude and slanderous political or social behaviors.

2. The most devastating effect of sin is that it puts a separation of sorts between God and us.
    a. Read again Isaiah 59:1–2 and summarize in your own words.

    b. Read Deuteronomy 32:19–20 and summarize.

c. There is no way for us to completely understand what it means for an omniscient, omnipresent God to be "separated" from anyone in all his creation. After the sin in the Garden of Eden, humankind was still in communication with God, and God was interacting and caring for them in ways. Perhaps we might get some idea of how this is possible by thinking of the regard loving parents maintain for a child who has left and refuses to have anything else to do with them. Considering the story Jesus told of the "Lost Son" might shed some light on the meaning of human separation from God (Luke 15:11–32). What do you think it means to be "separated from God" because of unforgiven sin?

d. The scripture does, however, draw a line of delineation between those who are saved and those who are not. Humankind and even modern Christianity have blurred these lines so as to make them socially and culturally unidentifiable. Clearly, scripture asserts that some belong to God and some do not, even though God still gives blessings even to those that do not know him, and he also sometimes allows his own children to suffer. God does not want anyone to perish, but in grace, he has given each of us the "free will" to in faith accept or reject his offer to save us (2 Pet. 3:9; 1 Tim. 2:4).

   i. In Matthew 7:21–23, Jesus predicts his sad pronouncement at judgment on "many" Christians whom Jesus says he will have never "known." What does this say about the separation that exists between God and those that are not "right" with him?

   ii. What does it say about the possibility that we might sincerely believe that we "know" him but that in reality he does not "know" us?

   iii. Read 2 Timothy 2:19. How does Paul's statement, along with the Matthew 7 text above, compare with the modern Christian notion that simply calling oneself Christians assures that one has a "right relationship" with God?

   iv. In John 14:6, Jesus says no one can come to (have access to) God the Father except through Christ. What are the implications then to those who are not seeking God through Jesus?

3. Sin is damaging, psychologically and emotionally.
   a. The Bible promises this: "You will keep in perfect peace those whose minds are steadfast, because they trust in you" (Isa. 26:3). There will be problems otherwise. What is "perfect peace"?

   b. Read Isaiah 48:17–18. Describe in your own words God's sad pronouncement to Israel because of their disobedience and sin.

   c. Consider each of the following passages, and write how sin and living apart from God damages us psychologically:
      i. 2 Timothy 3:1–5

      ii. 1 Timothy 4:1

      iii. Romans 1:18–32

      iv. Ephesians 4:17–19

   d. Mentally, sin damages us because it deceives us and causes us to believe lies. When the mind operates on things that are not true and fails to believe things that are, the results can range from simply bad to catastrophic. Think of some modern-day lies and deceptions that are currently proving psychologically damaging.

   e. The human mind needs truth to operate effectively. Read what Jesus said in John 8:31–32. What does the truth, as revealed by Jesus, do for us?

f. What do you think it means that the truth "sets us free"? Perhaps it would be helpful to consider how lies and deceptions enslave and imprison us.
_____
_____
_____

g. Emotionally, sin damages as well. Considering that there are at least four destructive emotion categories/cycles that people experience, list some ways sin causes harm in these areas.
   i. Egotism and self-centeredness:
   _____
   _____
   _____

   ii. Fear, anxiety, and apprehension:
   _____
   _____
   _____

   iii. Hate, anger, and hostility:
   _____
   _____
   _____

   iv. Sadness, guilt, depression:
   _____
   _____
   _____

h. Consider also some of the basic human emotional needs we all have and how sin can at least deprive us of these and at worst give us exactly the opposite.
   i. Love and affection:
   _____
   _____
   _____

   ii. Appreciation and affirmation:
   _____
   _____
   _____

   iii. Acceptance and a sense of belonging:
   _____
   _____
   _____

   iv. Purpose and achievement:
   _____
   _____
   _____

4. Sin can prove damaging to our bodies.
   a. "I pray that you may enjoy good health and that all may go well with you, even as your soul is getting along well" (3 John 2). Why do you think striving for good health is important to spirituality?
   _____
   _____
   _____

   b. Paul writes in 2 Corinthians 7:1, "let us purify ourselves from everything that contaminates body and spirit, perfecting holiness out of reverence for God." What do you think this passage means?
   _____
   _____
   _____

   c. Consider the mental or physical health implications of each of these passages:
      i. Exodus 23:25 _____
      ii. Exodus 15:26 _____
      iii. Deuteronomy 7:12–15 _____
      iv. Romans 12:1 _____
      v. 1 Corinthians 6:19–20 _____
      vi. 1 Corinthians 10:31 _____
      vii. 2 Corinthians 7:1 _____
      viii. James 5:14–15 _____

   d. Doctors consider stress, anxiety, depression, poor diet, lack of or too much exercise, tobacco use, excessive alcohol consumption, use of illegal or otherwise unhealthy drugs, and so forth to be root causes of or contributing factors to a significant amount of human disease and poor health. In what ways can the basic truths of scriptures help alleviate or prevent the root causes of these health issues?
   _____
   _____
   _____

   e. God also gives us wisdom if we seek it and ask for it (James 1:5). God gave mankind responsibility for the whole world (Gen. 1:28) not to mention our own health and well-being. How can gaining wisdom help us in all areas to make better decisions individually, socially, and culturally to improve the healthfulness of everyone, even in areas where scientific understanding is limited?
   _____
   _____
   _____

5. Sin is socially damaging.
   a. Jesus said to his people: "You are the salt of the earth. But if the salt loses its saltiness, how can it be made salty again? It is no longer good for anything, except to be thrown out and trampled underfoot. You are the light of the world. A town built on a hill cannot be hidden. Neither do people light a lamp and put it under a bowl. Instead they put it on its stand, and it gives light to everyone in the house. In the same way, let your light shine before others, that they may see your good deeds and glorify your

Father in heaven" (Matt. 5:13–16). How does it bless the world when Christians live out their purpose in the world of being salt and light?

b. Scripture contains plenty of instructions that directly impact areas of responsibilities all people have. As Christians, we are not always very good at applying these practices, and we as well as others, suffer for it. Truly following God's way protects against and brings healing to many social ills. Consider the areas below and the scripture next to each. How will applying God's Word to these areas protect against and heal the social damages caused by our sins?

　i.　Self-sacrifice, John 13:34–35

　ii.　Spiritual, Ephesians 4:17–32

　iii.　Moral, Ephesians 5:1–11

　iv.　Marriage, Ephesians 5:21–28

　v.　Parenting, Ephesians 6:1–4

　vi.　Community, Philippians 2:1–5

　vii.　Social responsibility, Philippians 2:1–5

viii. Human rights and dignity, Romans 12:10

ix. Welfare and care for the weak, Acts 20:35

x. Protection of individuals and societies, Romans 13:1–5

xi. Economic fairness, Proverbs 19:17; 22:16

xii. Peace, Romans 12:17–21

Self-Reflection

1. How clear is my present understanding of sin?

2. What new thoughts, teachings, or ideas did I learn from this lesson?

3. How has sin damaged my family, loved ones, and others?

4. How has sin negatively affected me?

5. Which sins do I personally struggle with the most?
   _____
   _____

6. What actions, if any, have I previously taken to repent or improve?
   _____
   _____

7. What actions might I need to take in regard to this lesson?
   _____
   _____
   _____

LESSON 5
"Jesus is Lord"

INTRODUCTION

If you declare with your mouth, "Jesus is Lord," and believe in your heart that God raised him from the dead, you will be saved. For it is with your heart that you believe and are justified, and it is with your mouth that you profess your faith and are saved. (Rom. 10:9–10)

"JESUS IS LORD" HAS LONG been the confession of faith for new believers, but confession is not the end goal, the reality of Jesus as the Lord of each of our lives is the ultimate goal (John 8:31; 1 Cor. 15:1). Belief *in* that confession as well as acceptance and application *of* it are both requirements for the true believer. A believer is one that lives by the reality that Jesus is Lord. It is this sincere confession that is required for salvation. To receive Jesus's salvation we must truly and sincerely accept him as Lord. Jesus is not just a good man. Jesus is not just some sort of divine Santa Claus sent to gratify our wants or to protect us from trouble. He does not seek to be just a good influence on us—he seeks to reign in our lives. Jesus is God's coming in the flesh to reestablish the relationship with mankind that was lost in the Fall in the Garden of Eden. The whole Bible is ultimately designed to get us to the point that we accept that not only is Jesus *the* Lord, but that we each individually surrender to him as *our* own Lord.

The Old Testament sets the stage by showing how it all began and how humankind became estranged from God. It shows the resulting Fall of Man due to the choice man and woman made in pursuing the Knowledge of Good and Evil over the Life—choosing self-reliance and trusting in self, rather than trusting in God. The Old Testament demonstrates our need for a savior by clearly showing humankind's complete inability to save ourselves through our own obedience and goodness. The Old Testament also establishes Jesus as the Messiah and Christ as well as the Lord of heaven and earth. By tracing the genealogies from Adam through Abraham through David all the way to Christ, and in addition seeing how the numerous prophecies concerning the Messiah were fulfilled in Jesus, the Old Testament verifies Jesus's true identity as the Messiah and our Lord!

However, the Bible unfortunately can itself become for us a Tree of the Knowledge of Good and Evil rather than the "Tree of Life." If we think that by having it "all figured out"—thinking that we are right with God because we are somehow "right" about things—we will repeat the same mistakes of legalism, pride, and self-reliance that Israel made and that many Christians and churches have also made over the centuries. Trusting in our doctrines, our churches, and ourselves, rather than trusting in God will lead us to the wrong tree, which brings death, rather than to the right tree—God—who alone can give us life. Finding God in the Bible requires finding Jesus, the Lord and creator of the universe and surrendering completely to him. The purpose of this lesson is for each person to be able to arrive at this conclusion and to make the decision that Jesus is Lord and that he is therefore *my* Lord!

Key Scripture: Genesis 3:15—God promised that a male from the seed of woman would crush Satan's head, symbolizing Satan's ultimate defeat.

1. This "Seed of Woman" promise was first given to Abraham (Gen. 12:1–3), then to Abraham's son Isaac (Gen. 26:2–4), and then to Isaac's son Jacob, whose name was changed to Israel (Gen. 28:14). When Jacob (Israel) blessed his son Judah, he indicated that the scepter (symbol of kingship) would pass to him rather than any of the other sons (Gen. 49:10). Most believe that this promised "Seed" of woman is ultimately fulfilled in Christ. Either way though, the Bible carefully establishes Jesus's lineage and the succession of the promise from Abraham to Jesus Christ. This lineage or "seed line" of Christ flows from Abraham through King David, who was from the tribe of Judah, and on to Mary and Joseph. In the Christmas story, we are reminded that Jesus was of the tribe of Judah, as predicted through prophecy. In your own words, why do you think God used a lineage or seed line as a key proof that Jesus of Nazareth was the promised Lord and Christ (Matt. 1:2–17)?

2. In Romans 16:20, Paul says, using the language of Genesis 3:15, that God would "crush Satan's head" under his feet. How do you see that God finally defeated Satan and his offspring (seed) through Eve and her offspring (seed)?

3. How do you think he defeats him in our individual lives today?

Further Study

1. Read Philippians 2:5–11. How does Paul say Jesus ultimately was exalted to the highest place?

    a. Why is that important for us?

    b. What does Paul say is the essential confession every person will finally make?

2. Read over Colossians 2:9–15 and consider the answers to these questions.
   a. What does Paul say about who Christ is (verses 9–10)?

   b. What are all the things he did for us then and still does for us today?

   c. How did God's removal of the written code (the Law) help us (see also Gal. 3:10–14)?

   d. In removing the law, how did he disarm the power of Satan, the accuser, and the other evil spirits (consider Rev. 12:10)?

   e. How in doing that did he defeat Satan (crush his head)?

3. Read and ponder Romans 8. Specifically, consider Romans 8:1–5, 28, 37–39. List as many things you can find that Paul says we have in Christ because of his victory over Satan?

Key Scripture: Galatians 3:19–29—Paul explains for us the relationship of the "Seed of Woman" promise, the coming of the Law of Moses, and the progression to faith in Christ with all its blessings.

1. What does Paul say the purpose of the Law of Moses was (verse 19)?

2. Why does Paul say the Law was instituted in the first place (verse 24)?

3. What do you suppose is the difference between being justified (made right with God) by Law and being justified by faith in Christ Jesus?

4. Why are we unable to be saved by the Law (see Gal. 3:10)?

5. How does the story of the Law's inability to save us (see verse 21) lead us to the faith to trust in Jesus as Lord?

6. How do we become sons of God (verses 26 and 27)?

7. What is our blessing when Jesus is our Lord and our Savior (verses 28 and 29)?

Further Study

1. In 1 Corinthians 10:1–13, Paul uses the experiences of the Israelites as a metaphor for our life as Christians.
    a. They were baptized by passing through the Red Sea (as are we baptized into Christ).
    b. They ate the "spiritual food," the manna that fell from heaven (just as we eat the bread in the Lord's Supper as well as ingest Jesus as the Bread of Life).
    c. They drank the water from the rock. Paul calls it the "spiritual drink" (referencing again our own participation in the Lord's Supper, as well as receiving the Holy Spirit from the rock, Christ).
    d. What are the examples and warnings Paul mentions from the Old Testament that are given to us as Christians?

2. In Romans 15:4, why does Paul say the things of the Old Testament were written down?

Key Scripture: Hebrews 8:6–13—The writer of Hebrews explained why the ministry and covenant of Jesus Christ replaced the Old Testament covenant that was based on the Law.

1. In the Bible there are two covenants revealed. The first was the covenant God made with the people of Israel after leading them out of Egypt (Exod. 19:1–8). This covenant basically said that if Israel would keep all of his commandments, he would give them their own land to live in, and that he would be their God and they his special people (verse 5). The commands are what comprise the Law of Moses, or often just called the Law. There are over six hundred laws in the Law of Moses, and as their part of the Old Covenant they simply could not violate even one single law or else they would have broken the whole covenant (James 2:10; Gal. 3:10–11). Therefore, why does the Book of Hebrews say a new covenant was made?

2. Read the quotation from the prophet Jeremiah in given in Hebrews 8:8–12 and summarize its messages.

3. What does verse 13 say was already happening at that time?

Further Study

1. Read Romans 7:1–6.
   a. As best you can, explain in your own words how in Christ humankind was released from the Law, allowing us to be "married" to Christ under a new covenant?

   b. As stated in verse 6, what does it mean then that we serve in the "new way of the Spirit" rather than in the old way of the written code (the Law)?

2. Read Galatians 3:1–14 and consider Paul's revelation concerning the Law and the New Covenant of Christ. What are the key points he makes in these verses?

Key Scripture: Colossians 2:8, 16–18—Paul explains that everything we do must be according to Christ's will rather than according to the Law, the basic principles and teachings of men, or mere human tradition.

1. Consider verse 8 of this text. What does it mean to do everything "according to Christ" or "depending on Christ"?

2. What are the things that Paul says can take us "captive" and lead us from being obedient to Jesus as Lord?

3. What does it mean in this context to be taken captive by certain teachings?

4. In Mark 7:9, how did Jesus say the Jews misused their own traditions in regard to the will of God?

5. In Matthew 10:37–38, how did Jesus compare allegiance to him with allegiance to even our own parents?

6. Notice in Colossians 2:16–18 the things that are said to be "shadows" (foreshadows) of things to come and what the reality actually is (see figure 6 below). This language is referring to how it is to see someone's shadow before you see the actual person. The shadow in that case is a "fore" shadow of the person to come. The person though is the real thing. What are the implications of this to the Old Testament and the New Testament?

Further Study

1. Jesus embodied the Law and was in fact Lord of it.
    a. Note in Matthew 5:20 of the Sermon on the Mount, how he commanded their righteousness to exceed that of the rigid law-keeping Pharisees. Given the tremendous efforts these devoted Jews had in keeping the law, how could anybody expect to exceed them in righteousness?

b. In the scripture there are two kinds of righteousness. The first has to do with living right according to the will of God. The second is when God assigns to us the righteousness of Christ, seeing us as holy and blameless (Rom. 1:16–17; Eph. 1:4). With that in mind, what might Jesus be speaking of in regard to righteousness?

_____
_____

c. Paul says Jesus provided the way for us to be righteous by his own exact obedience to the Law. He then assigned his perfection to those of us that have faith in him (Rom. 8:1–5). What do you think it means that Jesus assigned his perfection or righteousness to us?

_____
_____

d. How should the reality that we start out our life in Christ being seen already as perfect in God's sight affect the efforts we make to then live righteous lives according to the will and ways of God?

_____
_____

e. Read Romans 1:16–17 and Philippians 3:8–9. Through Jesus's keeping of the Law and dying for our sins, we have this new kind of "righteousness." Where does this new righteousness come from and what is our role in it?

_____
_____

2. Read Matthew 12:1–14, noting in verse 8 that Jesus declared himself as "Lord of the Sabbath." The Sabbath was to the Jews one of the most important laws. It is the fourth of the Ten Commandments (Exod. 20:8–10). Notice that Jesus sets himself above the Law in this passage and in fact is the original giver of it. Who does Jesus say he is in regard to the Sabbath (and by inference the whole law), and what does that mean?

_____
_____

3. The dietary laws of the Jews were given to them as a practicality to help keep them from having the diseases that could be caught from eating "unclean" meats and foods. The Jews took great personal pride in how this distinguished them from others. However, in Mark 7:1–23, Jesus overturns this important law. Note in verse 19 what Jesus declares. How does he again show himself as over and above the Law that they so revered?

_____
_____

Figure 6: Some of the "Shadows" of the Old Testament and the "Realities" of the New Testament

Old Testament		New Testament
Israel	**Nation**	Believers
Egypt	**Bondage**	Sin
Moses	**Deliverer**	Jesus
Sacrificial Offerings	**Blood of Lamb**	Blood of Jesus
Passover	**Feast**	Communion
Wilderness	**Journey**	Life
Manna	*Physical* **Bread** *Spiritual*	Jesus
Temple Mount	**Rock**	Jesus
Meribah	**Water from the Rock**	Holy Spirit
Canaan	**Promised Land**	Heaven
Flood/Red Sea	**Rebirth/Water**	Baptism
Jerusalem	**Temple**	Heart

SELF-REFLECTION

1. How persuasive do I see the Old Testament to be in demonstrating to me that Jesus is truly the promised Messiah and Christ, and thus to be my Lord?

   _____
   _____
   _____

2. How has studying this lesson affected my views on Jesus?

   _____
   _____
   _____

3. What is the most important lesson I learned?
   _____
   _____

4. How can understanding the shadows of the Old Testament and the corresponding realities of the New Testament help in my overall understanding of discovering Jesus?
   _____
   _____

5. What one action will I take in regard to this lesson?
   _____
   _____

LESSON 6
Discovering Jesus

Introduction

Here I am! I stand at the door and knock. If anyone hears my voice and opens the door, I will come in and eat with that person, and they with me. (Jesus Christ, Rev. 3:20)

Seek and you will find. (Jesus Christ, Matt. 7:7)

The first thing Andrew did, after meeting Jesus, was to find his brother Simon and tell him, "We have found the Messiah" (that is, the Christ). And he brought him to Jesus. (John 1:41–42)

"We have found the Messiah," Andrew said. Have you found Christ? Have you discovered Jesus? Each generation of the faithful Jews had been looking for the Messiah, especially since the Babylonian Exile period, when they had been torn from the Promised Land and many were taken to faraway places as captives. The Jews were generally very patriotic, with an intense love for their country. They hated being ruled by Rome. Their predominant view of the promised Messiah was that he would be a king like King David who would lead them to independence and even to great conquests. Sadly though, as Isaiah prophesied and as the apostle John noted, when Christ finally came, the nation as a whole rejected him as their Messiah (Isa. 53:1; John 1:11)! The prophet Isaiah said, "He was despised and rejected by mankind, a man of suffering, and familiar with pain. Like one from whom people hide their faces he was despised, and we held him in low esteem" (Isa. 53:3). He was not who or what they expected—or even wanted for that matter. The prophets predicted his rejection by his own people, the nation of Israel. We as humans, in our fleshly natures, have a tendency, when we get desperate for something, to actually reject or drive away the very things we are so desperate for, once those things come into view. Perhaps in our desperation we fear it is perhaps too good to be true! Maybe it was not what we wanted it to be. Or are we just doubtful (lacking faith) a lot of the times?

Furthermore, the Bible asserts that ultimately every human shares in the rejection and crucifixion of Christ—that we are all guilty of this crime. If it is to be said that Adam and Eve's sin in the Garden of Eden was the original sin, then it certainly can also be said that the rejection and crucifixion of Christ, by all humanity, is the ultimate sin. Worse than simply choosing the Tree of the Knowledge of Good and Evil, in the crucifixion, mankind rejected the Tree of Life!

By God's own plan and foreknowledge, humankind has again been given an opportunity to reject the forbidden tree and to once and for all choose the Tree of Life—Jesus. And the Bible is clear—to find and choose Jesus is to find and choose God, and to find and choose God is to find and choose Jesus (John 14:6–11). "If you have seen me, you have seen the Father" (Jesus, John 14:9). "This is my Son, whom I love; with him I am well pleased. Listen to him!" (God speaking from heaven, Matt. 17:5). As we read in the New Testament, many rejected him. However, many also found him. John said, "He came to that which was his own, but his own did not receive him. Yet to all who did receive him, to those who believed in his name, he gave the right to become children of God" (John 1:11–12).

To find Jesus is to find God, and he gives us, through Jesus, the right to become his children. This lesson is designed to encourage further the seeking out and finding of Jesus—discovering Jesus!

Key Scripture: John 20:19–29—The first step in discovering Jesus is recognizing and believing in him for who he is—Our Lord and God!

1. It is hard to imagine all that the original twelve apostles saw and heard. It is hard to imagine their thoughts, their fears, their amazement, and their doubts as they followed Jesus over the three or so years they were with him. In the scripture above, we see John's account of Jesus's appearance to the apostles after he had been brutally crucified and buried, and then their having found his burial tomb empty. When they looked in the tomb, his body was gone and the burial cloths were still lying there. The first time he appeared to the apostles together after his death, Thomas was not present and understandably refused to believe the resurrection had occurred, unless he said he actually saw and touched Jesus himself. The second time Jesus appeared to the apostles, Thomas was there. Jesus again appeared out of nowhere. Describe in your own words the response of Thomas when he encountered the resurrected Christ.

2. Why was it so hard for them to believe that Jesus was indeed from God after all they had seen and done?

3. Why is it even harder for us to believe it today?

4. However, because something is hard to believe does not mean it is not true. Think of all the unbelievable things that have happened through history, or all of the discovered truths of our universe. If there was not strong evidence concerning them, most would of course not believe them. Give an example.

5. Do you believe there is in fact anything God could have done then or could still do now that would unequivocally, once and for all, convince everyone that Jesus was and is indeed the Son of God who came to save the world? Why or why not?

6. Why do you suppose that God chose to offer us salvation through our believing the evidence given to us that Jesus was indeed God in the flesh, that he died and rose for our sins, and that he intercedes for us continually with God, and then accepting him by faith as our own Lord and Savior?

7. Describe how each of us might experience in our own lives what Thomas experienced in his—fully recognizing Jesus as our Lord and God—and how it should impact us.

8. What did Jesus say was to come to those of us who were not there to actually see him but who still believe in him as the resurrected Christ?

Further Study

1. Review 2 Peter 1:16–21. Here Peter gives his own testimony as an eyewitness of Jesus and as an authority on the reality that Jesus was and is the Christ. What is his testimony, and why might it be considered believable?

2. Think of a few significant historical events that we accept as true based on eyewitness accounts and "authorities" on various subjects.

3. What makes some witnesses more believable than others?

4. What does the judicial phrase "beyond a reasonable doubt" mean, and how does it apply here?

5. If the early disciples had, for any reason, fabricated the stories about Jesus's divinity, and especially his resurrection, do you think they would have suffered and died the way they did when their confessions of what they saw would inevitably lead to hopeless and brutal deaths? Why or why not?
   _____
   _____

6. Read Hebrews 11:1, 6. Hebrews says faith is about confidence in our hope (biblical hope is an expectation, not just a wish) and an assurance of what we believe in but cannot see. Confidence is faith. Assurance is about the depth of conviction. Assurance produces hope. Why do you suppose it is impossible to please God, or to find Jesus, without such faith?
   _____
   _____

7. Hebrews 11 chronicles the legacy of faith of the people we read about in the Bible. Take the time to read this most inspiring chapter. The apostle Paul says that as Christians we all "walk by faith and not by sight" (2 Cor. 5:7).
   a. Why might it be said that everyone—whether a believer in God or not—lives by faith every day?
   _____
   _____

   b. Why can it be said that everyone lives by faith in something?
   _____
   _____

   c. How many important things can you think of that we all believe in but cannot see?
   _____
   _____

   d. How many important things do we accept as true without personally validating them (such as validating your own doctor's medical degree before you accept treatment from her/him!)?
   _____
   _____

   e. Why do we accept atomic theory or the existence of microbes when we cannot see them with our own unassisted eyes?
   _____
   _____

   f. Why do we believe in dark matter, which comprises over 90 percent of all matter, and we cannot find it or see it?
   _____
   _____

g. Or why do we accept the existence of gravity when science cannot even figure out where it comes from but only sees its effects?

h. Why do we accept the truth of the existence of any historical figure that has passed?

i. Why do we believe in the existence of our own ancestors whom we have personally never met or seen?

j. Is there faith involved in scientific hypotheses or theories? If so, why?

8. Faith is essential in all our personal relationships. Marriage itself is a "faith relationship." We must trust that our chosen mates are sincere in their intentions and vows, even though we cannot see into their minds and hearts. Only time will tell the real tale of what is inside of them. We must trust our mates are being faithful to us even when we are not actually present with them. We generally have no easy way of knowing for sure if they are or are not, unless of course we want to have them constantly monitored. A measure of faith is required in all our relationships, and a substantial amount of faith is essential to those relationships that we cherish most. How do you see that faith is in fact essential to a quality life and to good relationships?

9. Faith even keeps us connected in our hearts to those we loved who have passed on. We cannot see them, but we believe they did once exist in our lives, and most of us believe they still exist in another way in another place. Do you believe this kind of faith to be illogical or unreasonable? Why or why not?

10. Why might it be said that it is impossible, in reality, to *not* live by faith—at least faith in some things or persons?

Key Scripture: John 20:30–31—The next step is to make a decision concerning Jesus and live out our lives in his name—by his authority!

11. The Bible is not written as a storybook. The Bible is not written simply as a book of religion, or a book of inspiration. The apostle John in his gospel did not write a nice, readable biography of Jesus for our reading enjoyment. As noted in the scripture above, why did John say he had written his account of Christ?
    _____
    _____

12. The "miraculous signs" that John refers to in this verse are the seven miracles Jesus performed that John tells us about in his gospel. In all, it is said that Jesus performed thirty-seven miracles (counting the ones in the other three gospel accounts) plus the miracle of the resurrection itself that was performed on him by God the Father. Consider John's record of Jesus's miracles and make a note after each about what it might be showing us about Jesus.
    a. John 2:1–11—Jesus changes water to wine at the wedding of some family friends. Mary calls him to do it, clearly knowing already his ability to perform such miracles.
       _____
       _____

    b. John 4:43–54—Jesus heals an important official's son. He actually heals the boy from afar, and John tells us the boy's whole family became believers!
       _____
       _____

    c. John 6:1–5—Jesus manages to feed a crowd of five thousand people starting with only five small loaves of bread and two fish, and has twelve basketsful of fish left over after everyone had eaten!
       _____
       _____

    d. John 6:16–25—After miraculously feeding the hungry crowd, Jesus sends the apostles out in a boat while he disperses the crowd. Then he walks out to the boat on the surface of the water!
       _____
       _____

    e. John 9:1–41—Jesus miraculously heals a man born blind. Note the details that John shares in the story involving quite a few others. Notice the means Jesus uses to bring about the healing—mud in the eyes and washing in a particular pool (why would someone make this kind of stuff up?!).
       _____
       _____

f. John 11:1–44—Jesus raises his friend Lazarus from the dead after he had been dead and buried for four days! Again, note the real people in the story and the details John gives. These are details that could have easily been refuted at the time by others if the story or its details were suspect.

g. Additionally John tells us about Jesus's own resurrection (John 19 and 20), and as well as a miraculous catch of fish that Jesus brings about afterward (John 21:1–14).

13. Consider each miracle and what need or provision it assures us that Jesus can provide. Note that these cover the gamut of human needs: social, health, food, abilities, sight, and life itself. John concludes his gospel saying that the world could not contain all the books that would have to be written if everything Jesus had done were to be written down (John 21:25). How should all of this give us more confidence about the claims about Jesus?

14. What do these miracles, along with the array of other stories about Jesus, tell us about the heart and character of Jesus, and how can they help us not only "find" him but also know and experience him personally in this present life?

15. Are these miracles enough to cause us to believe that Jesus was and is indeed the Christ, the Son of God? If not, what more could God have done or do to prove it to you?

16. How can knowing and believing these miracles lead us to a personal faith relationship with him, even though he is not with us in bodily form?

17. Doing anything in another's name is to have his or her "authority" to do it, such as in the case of someone giving another the "Power of Attorney." How does knowing about and believing in Jesus's power and authority cause us to want to "have life in *His* name" (see also Matt. 28:18–20)?

Further Study

1. John reveals the significant claims Christ made about himself. These take the form of "I am" statements. The statement "I am" harkens back to the very name or description of himself that God revealed to Moses after Moses asked God who he should tell Pharaoh had sent him (Exod. 3:13–14). God calls himself "I am who I am," rendered or transliterated as *Yahweh* or *Jehovah*. In John 8:58, we read that Jesus said, "Before Abraham was, *I am*." Note these examples of who Jesus says he is, and what the implication is of each. Jesus said, "I am…"

    a. The Messiah, John 4:26

    b. The Bread of Life, John 6:35

    c. From Above, John 8:23

    d. The Eternal One, John 8:58

    e. The Light of the World, John 9:5

    f. The Gate (or Door), John 10:7

    g. The Son of God, John 10:36

    h. The Resurrection and the Life, John 11:25

i. The Teacher and Lord, John 13:13

j. The Way, Truth, and Life, John 14:6

k. The True Vine, John 15:1

2. It has long been observed, that based on all we have recorded about him, Jesus could only have been the Son of God, otherwise he was a liar or a mad man. Many want to historically redefine him as simply a good or wise man whose disciples made him out to be more than he really was. Consider each option below concerning the possible choices of who he was. What are the strengths and weaknesses in favor of each argument based on the evidence available?

   a. The Son of God

   b. A liar

   c. A mad man

   d. Just a good man

Key Scripture: Philippians 3:10—The third step in finding Jesus is getting to know him personally.

1. Read Philippians 3:1–14. How do we see that Christ was indeed very real to Paul?

a. The word "know" can mean to be acquainted with someone intellectually, as well as to know someone experientially and personally.
   i. What do you think it means to know Christ intellectually?

   _____
   _____

   ii. What do you think it means to know Christ experientially and personally?

   _____
   _____

   iii. Which do you think Paul was talking about in verse 10?

   _____
   _____

b. When Paul wrote Philippians, he had already been in a close, personal relationship with Christ for many years. Given his knowledge and experience of Christ, what worth does Paul put on knowing Christ, and continuing to know him better (read also Phil. 1:21–22)?

   _____
   _____

c. What possible reasons could Paul, as one that had paid such a supreme price for following Christ, have possibly had for giving up everything to know Christ and even see it as a blessing to participate in Christ's suffering and death? Can you think of one other than that he was fully convinced by what he saw and heard directly from Jesus (verse 10)?

   _____
   _____

2. We can know and experience Jesus through the Creation (he is after all its Creator), through the Word of God (he revealed it), through his church (it is his body), and through the Holy Spirit (the Spirit of God through whom Jesus now comes to us). As you think through each, consider why it is important to take the time to know Jesus through all of these rather than just one or two of them.

3. Knowing God through the Creation.
   a. First, read Colossians 1:15-20. In this text, Paul explains the supremacy of Christ over Creation. In the space provided list the things he says that Jesus is and what you think each one means (use a Bible dictionary or commentary if necessary). Depending on how specific you get, you might list more or less than the blanks provided.

   _____
   _____
   _____
   _____
   _____

b. Read Romans 1:20. The apostle Paul says that "God's invisible qualities—his eternal power and divine nature" are clearly seen and understood through the things that Jesus created. In that Jesus is the designer and engineer, the builder, the architect, the artist, and the sustainer of the universe, what are some qualities of his eternal power and divinity that we can surmise through the Creation, and how will they draw us into a closer and more personal experience of him?

4. Knowing Christ through the Word.
   a. Consider these passages concerning the Word *of* God and the Creation.
      i. John 1:1–2 reveals to us that Jesus is the Word of God.
      ii. Psalms 33:6–9 reveals that by the Lord's Word the world came into existence.
      iii. Hebrews 1:3 reveals to us that Jesus sustains the world through his powerful Word.
      iv. Colossians 1:17 reveals to us that Jesus holds the world together through his powerful Word.
      v. How then can we experience Jesus as the Word in the Creation itself?

b. Consider these passages concerning the words *from* God in the Bible, making a note or two after each concerning how you feel it applies to our experience of Jesus through the Word.
   i. In John 14:26, Jesus told the apostles that he would bring everything he had taught them to their remembrance.
   _____
   _____
   _____

   ii. In John 16:13, Jesus said he would send the Spirit to guide them into "all truth."
   _____
   _____
   _____

   iii. In 2 Peter 1:16–21, Peter asserted that his writing was eyewitness testimony, that in Christ the prophecies were validated, and that everyone would do well to pay attention to its reality.
   _____
   _____
   _____

   iv. In 2 Peter 3:16, Peter calls Paul's writing "scripture." How does Peter's testimony then validate Paul's testimony and writing?
   _____
   _____
   _____

   v. In 1 Corinthians 14:37, Paul declared his writing as the "Lord's commandments."
   _____
   _____
   _____

   vi. In 1 Thessalonians 2:13, Paul commended the Thessalonians for receiving his message not just as Paul's words but as he said it was—the Word of God."
   _____
   _____
   _____

   vii. Review Lesson 1, figure 3 and consider how we can find and experience Jesus through the written words *from* God found in the Bible that reveal the Word *of* God, Jesus the Son of God?
   _____
   _____
   _____

c. Given that the Word of God—Jesus—reveals himself through the words from God—the scriptures, how can we discover and come to know and experience Jesus through the Bible?
   _____
   _____
   _____

5. Knowing Christ through the Holy Spirit.
   a. In John 14:15–23, Jesus said that if anyone obeys his commands (obviously speaking of those found in scripture), that Jesus would come and make his home with them—that he will be in us and with us through the Holy Spirit.
   b. In Matthew 28:19–20, Jesus said he would be with the apostles and the church through the ages as we continue to carry out his mission.
   c. In John 14:15–23; 15:26–27; 16:5–13; Luke 11:13; 24:49; Acts 1:4–8; and others, Jesus said he would send his Holy Spirit to love, lead, guide, convict, and reveal him to the apostles. Given these promises, how do you see that we can experience Jesus by his Holy Spirit within us as well?

   _____
   _____

   i. As Christians, we individually are temples of the Holy Spirit (Acts 2:38; 1 Cor. 6:19). What do you think this means?

   _____
   _____

   ii. Collectively, as Christ's church, we are a temple of the Holy Spirit (Eph. 2:21–22). What does this mean?

   _____
   _____

   d. In John 7:37–29, Jesus said the Holy Spirit would flow from believers. How do you think this works?

   _____
   _____

   e. In Romans 8:14–16, Paul writes that the Holy Spirit leads us as God's children and gives us the spirit and sense of our "sonship." How do you suppose the Holy Spirit makes us God's children and gives us this sense of being God's children?

   _____
   _____

   f. Further, in Romans 8:26–27, Paul tells us that the Holy Spirit helps us in our weaknesses, searches our hearts, and intercedes for us with God. How can understanding and seeking this relationship through the Spirit lead us in our daily experience of Jesus?

   _____
   _____

6. Knowing Christ through the church (the church as being the body of Christ is covered more thoroughly in Lesson 11).
   a. In Matthew 16:18, Jesus promised that he would himself build his church.
      i. He has and is doing this by drawing men and women to him as disciples and joining them together in him.
      ii. He works through the church to grow the church, numerically and spiritually.
      iii. How should it affect my way of thinking and regarding the church when I come to the realization that it is Christ that is building it not mere human efforts?
      _____
      _____
      _____

   b. Paul said concerning believers or Christians, "Now you are the body of Christ, and each one of you is a part of it" (1 Cor. 12:27).
      i. The church is the embodiment of Christ on earth in all of its imperfections, displaying his grace and mercy (Eph. 2:6–7).
      ii. The Holy Spirit personally "baptizes" each believer into Christ's body (1 Cor. 12:13).
      iii. It is Christ who is the bond that holds us together in peace and harmony (Eph. 2:14).
      iv. It is the Holy Spirit that unifies us and keeps us that way (Eph. 4:3). Ours is but to maintain that unity by the Spirit.
      v. Describe in your own words the significance of the reality that the church is the literal body of Christ?
      _____
      _____
      _____
      vi. How should this affect our attitude to the church Jesus is building?
      _____
      _____
      _____

   c. According to Paul, Christ said individual believers were "being built" together as a temple of the Holy Spirit. How do you suppose that Christ builds each of us into the church?
   _____
   _____
   _____

   d. What do you think each of our roles is in being built into the body?
   _____
   _____
   _____

   e. Knowing and experiencing Christ in community.
      i. In Acts 2:42–47, how does Luke describe the attributes of the first church community.
      _____
      _____
      _____

ii. How, when a community functions like this, will we experience Christ himself in it?
_____
_____

f. Knowing and experiencing Christ through the Lord's Supper (Communion) and church assemblies.
   i. In 1 Corinthians 11:17–34, Paul describes the serious nature of the communion, the Lord's Supper, as instituted by Jesus (Matt. 26:26–28).
      1) Jesus said the bread *is* his body and the cup *is* his blood. Any interpretation you may have of this must take into consideration the serious nature of the Lord's Supper.
      2) Paul strongly cautions the Corinthian church about participating in an unworthy manner, verse 27. What does he say the danger is of doing so?
      _____
      _____
      _____

      3) In verse 29, what does Paul say that those that eat without "discerning" the body of Christ are doing to themselves ("discerning the body of Christ" means acknowledging that the members of the church I am participating with are all part of the body of Christ and that Christ lives in them as well)?
      _____
      _____
      _____

      4) In your own words, how can we experience Christ through the Lord's Supper and Christian assembly?
      _____
      _____
      _____

g. Knowing and experiencing Christ through mutual ministry.
   i. Christ works through his church to minister to the church.
   ii. In 1 Corinthians 12:12–27, Paul discusses at length the interconnectedness within the body of Christ. What are some of the points he makes, and how do they collectively allow us to experience Christ in the church?
   _____
   _____
   _____

   iii. Lesson 11 of this series covers how Christians in the church are to build each other up. There are quite a number of commands concerning what we are to do for *one another*. What are some of the things you might be able to think of that we are instructed to do to and for one another, and how through these can we experience Christ in the church by both giving and receiving such blessings?
   _____
   _____
   _____

Further Study

1. In Acts 9:1–19 (also recounted in Acts 22 and 26), we read about Paul's conversion (he had previously been known as Saul). How real did the resurrected Christ seem to Paul according to this account and his subsequent testimonies about it?
   _____
   _____

2. In 2 Timothy 4:16–18, how real did Christ seem to Paul even at the very end of his life?
   _____
   _____

3. What is the personality of Jesus like? Read the following descriptions. There are seemingly countless examples of each of the characteristics of Christ in the stories about him. But here are just some statements and examples to get you started. After each make a note or two how we can experience these through the body of Christ.
    a. Jesus is incredibly loving and kind, Titus 3:4–5; John 13:34–35.
       _____
       _____

    b. Jesus is incredibly compassionate, Matthew 9:36.
       _____
       _____

    c. Jesus is incredibly humble, Philippians 2:5–11.
       _____
       _____

    d. Jesus is incredibly good, Acts 10:38, John 21:25.
       _____
       _____

    e. Jesus is incredibly powerful, Matthew 28:18; Mark 4:35–41.
       _____
       _____

    f. Jesus is incredibly driven and mission oriented, Mark 1:35–39; John 14:31.
       _____
       _____

g. Jesus is incredibly determined, Luke 9:51.

h. Jesus is incredibly honest and truthful, John 14:6.

i. Jesus is incredibly bold, Luke 11:37–41.

j. Jesus is incredibly sociable, Matthew 11:18–19.

k. Jesus is incredibly personable, John 11:33–36.

l. Jesus is incredibly faithful and trustworthy, Revelation 1:5.

m. Jesus is incredibly strong, John 16:33.

n. Jesus is incredibly real, John 20:30–31.

4. Who does the Bible say Jesus was and is? There are many ways Jesus is described in the scripture, but these are some of the major ones that show the scope of his identity in heaven and on earth. What is the implication of each of these?

   a. Son of God, John 1:49

b. Son of Man, John 1:51

c. Savior of the World, John 4:42

d. Christ/Messiah, John 1:41

e. Lamb of God, John 1:29

f. Lord and God, John 20:28

g. Fullness of Deity/God, Colossians 2:9

Key Scripture: John 18–20—Lastly we must come face-to-face with all that is revealed about God through the death, the burial and the resurrection of Christ.

1. Take the time in one setting to read this story. It summarizes the essence of what is often simply called "the Cross" or "the crucifixion" (see also, Matt. 26–28; Mark 14–16; and Luke 22–24 for the other three gospel accounts). What overall thoughts and emotions do you experience in reading this story?

2. Trying to adequately capture the essence of the death, burial, and resurrection of Christ is formidable, let alone trying to completely capture the depth of its meaning.
   a. However, for one to finally simply accept the good news, one must come face-to-face with the reality of the sufficiency of the Cross of Christ. Through our faith in what Jesus did, we can be fully restored in our relationships with God.
   b. Think through this account, and try with all of you heart to see every detail in your mind's eye. Picture him looking at you. See him as an incredibly loving father who died to protect you—the one he loves and planned to save from the foundation of the world.

    c. You might want to watch one of the movies about Christ, especially one that focuses on the whole series of events leading up to and surrounding Jesus's death on the cross. One that is particularly moving and true to scripture is *The Passion of Christ* (2004).

    d. As you read, watch, and ponder, try to personalize Christ's love, his passion, and his commitment to saving you. No love like this had ever been seen before nor has it ever been seen since.

    e. Write some reflections you might have as you read the account or take the time to watch one of the more biblically accurate movies.
_____
_____
_____

3. Consider John 15:13. Jesus says there is no greater expression of one's love for others than to die for them. What more could God have possibly done to demonstrate his love for us?
_____
_____
_____

Further Study

1. Read Romans 5:1–11. In this text, Paul comments on our being declared justified (forgiven) before God by faith in what Jesus did for us. What are the points the apostle makes here?
_____
_____

2. Read Hebrews 7:23–27, then consider what the scripture means when it says that Jesus can completely (forever) save those who put their faith in him!
_____
_____

3. Read the following scriptures about the Cross of Christ. What is the significance of each?
    a. Paul said it was the cross that he preached, 1 Corinthians 1:17.
_____
_____
_____

    b. Gloried in the cross, Galatians 6:14.
_____
_____
_____

    c. Reconciled through the cross, Ephesians. 2:16.
_____
_____
_____

d. Peace made by the cross, Colossians 1:20.

e. Law abolished by the cross, Colossians 2:14.

f. Christ came to save sinners by the cross, 1 Timothy 1:15.

4. The scripture says that in our conversions that we too are crucified—with Christ!
    a. Paul said that he (and by implication "we") have been crucified with Christ, Galatians 2:20. What do you think this means?

    b. The apostle Paul says that in each of our baptisms the old person is crucified with Christ, Romans 6:3–11. What is our part in this and what is God's part?

    c. Jesus in fact calls us to take up our own crosses daily in order to follow him, Luke 9:23. What do you think this means?

5. The New Testament puts particular emphasis on the effect of the blood of Christ in the removal of our sin. Consider these verses and what each may mean.
    a. In Matthew 26:28, Jesus says, "This is my blood of the covenant."

    b. In Acts 20:28, the apostle Paul told the Elders at Ephesus that Jesus had bought the church with his own blood.

    c. In Romans 5:9, Paul writes that we are justified (made just before God) by Jesus's blood.

d. In Hebrews 9:14, we are told that Jesus's blood cleanses our consciences from all of our sin.

e. In 1 Peter 1:18–19, Peter writes that we are redeemed (bought back or ransomed) by Christ's blood.

f. In 1 John 1:7, we are told that as we walk with Christ, it is his blood that continuously keeps us cleansed before God. Paul says that God, in fact, chooses to see us as though we are "holy and blameless" in Christ (Eph. 1:4).

g. In Revelation 1:5, we read that Christ has freed us from our sin by his own blood.

h. In Revelation 7:14, we read that as the redeemed, we "wash our robes" in his blood so that we stand before him clean and white!

i. Read Leviticus 17:11. Without getting into all the meanings behind the Old Testament sacrificial system, do you suppose God might have originally created living creatures and humans with blood to sustain them inwardly with the very intention of later using Jesus's blood, representing his own life, to give life to us?

Key Scripture: 1 John 2:3–6—The apostle John said that if we are to make the claim that we are Christians, or disciples, we must obey Christ, living as he lived.

1. To do what Jesus did, we must become like him in our character. To imitate him in character, we must come to better understand his character. How would you define what "character" is?

2. Read Philippians 2:5–8. Paul said we must have the same attitude of Christ. How does he describe Jesus's attitude?

3. In 2 Corinthians 3:18, Paul discusses Moses's encounter with God on Mt. Sinai. After this encounter with God, recorded in the Old Testament (Exod. 34:29), Moses came down the mountain with his face aglow. Paul goes on to say that the same thing happens to us as we "behold" and live in a relationship with Christ. What else does the apostle Paul say happens to us?

4. Who makes our transformations happen?

5. The Bible is full of descriptions of Jesus. Why is it important for each Christian to strive to truly behold him and to have a clear view of who Jesus is?

6. Review again who the scripture says that Jesus is and write out your own generalized description of the person and character of Christ.

Further Study

1. Read and consider Ephesians 5:1–2. How does a beloved child imitate her/his parents?

    a. How might it change your life for you to imitate God as a dearly loved child of his?

    b. What kind of life does Paul say for us then to live when we imitate him, and what does that tell us about the character and nature of God?

2. Read Romans 12:1–2 in conjunction with Ephesians 5:2.
    a. What does it mean that Christ "gave himself up for us"?

b. How do we then give ourselves up for God?

3. Read Phil 2:5–9. What is "attitude" and how does Paul describe Christ's attitude?

   a. Can you think of instances in Jesus's life where you see these attitude traits exemplified?

   b. How do you think your attitude needs to change to be more like Christ's?

Self-Reflection

1. Jesus once asked the apostles, after they had been with him nearly three years, "Who do you say I am?" Peter answered for all of them, saying, "You are the Messiah, the Son of the living God" (Matt. 16:15–16). Write out a statement in your own words who you believe Jesus is.

2. Why do the eyewitness accounts of Jesus's life, miracles, and resurrection form a compelling case for the reality of who he claimed to be—the Christ?

3. Based on the eyewitness accounts of Jesus's personality and character, write out your own personal description of how you see him.

4. Write in your own words the implications of the crucifixion of Christ to you.

5. Based on what you have studied so far, describe what do you think it means to "walk as Jesus did" in your own life today.
   _____
   _____
   _____

6. Write in your own words how you can discover Jesus through the Bible, the creation, the church, and the Holy Spirit.
   _____
   _____
   _____

7. If Jesus was and is who he claimed to be, what are the main blessings that come to you and others for finding him and walking with him?
   _____
   _____
   _____

8. There is a song that was written by Mark Altrogge in 1987 called "I Stand in Awe of You." It can easily be heard by various artists on YouTube and other places. Take some time to read the words, possibly listen to it, and ponder the idea of standing in awe of one as beautiful as Jesus Christ. Write out your own thoughts and reflections afterward. The lyrics are as follows.

(verse 1)
You are beautiful beyond description,
Too marvelous for words,
Too wonderful for comprehension,
Like nothing ever seen or heard.
Who can grasp your infinite wisdom?
Who can fathom the depth of your love?
You are beautiful beyond description,
Majesty enthroned above.

(Chorus)
And I stand, I stand in awe of you.
I stand, I stand in awe of you.
Holy God, to whom all praise is due,
I stand in awe of you.

(verse 2)
You are beautiful beyond description,
Yet God crushed You for my sin,
In agony and deep affliction,

Cut off that I might enter in.
Who can grasp such tender compassion?
Who can fathom this mercy so free?
You are beautiful beyond description,
Lamb of God, Who died for me.

Write your own personal reflections and praises on beholding God through Jesus.
_____
_____
_____

LESSON 7
Accepting Jesus as Your Lord: Discipleship

Introduction

When Jesus began his ministry, his call to the disciples was simply, "Follow me..." (Matt. 4:19–20 and Luke 9:23). The apostle John said that the test of the authenticity of our Christian life was not in what we claimed or thought but rather, "Whoever claims to live in him must live as Jesus did" (1 John 2:6). Jesus said that many are invited but few chosen (Matt. 22:14). Jesus said that few rather than many would find life (Matt. 7:13–14). In fact, he said that not everyone who called him Lord would be saved, saying that many who had called him Lord and done "Christian" works would find, in the end, that they had never even been saved. Sadly, he will say to these, "I never knew you" (Matt. 7:21–23).

Thus while it is easy to see in scripture the essentiality of actually following and obeying Jesus, many live out their Christianity or religious commitment casually with far too little seriousness or self-examination. Many are more devoted to their traditions than they are to Christ. Many seem more intent on justifying themselves than they are in letting God justify them. They are often captive to particular interpretations, denominations, personal desires, or beliefs that they put their confidence in, rather than seeking solely to follow Jesus in life, faith, and doctrine.

This lesson is designed to explain biblically to a new student of Christianity what the Bible calls true faith and obedience. It is also meant to challenge those of us that already call ourselves Christians to do as Paul commanded in 2 Corinthians 13:5: "Examine yourselves to see whether you are in the faith; test yourselves. Do you not realize that Christ Jesus is in you—unless, of course, you fail the test?"

Don't fail.

Key Scripture: John 14:6—Accepting Jesus for who he is.

1. Jesus taught that he is the *way to God*, the *truth of God*, the *life from God*, and that there is no other way to God. Jesus leaves no honest choices but to either accept him all the way or to reject him all the way. Consider each of the words: "way," "truth," and "life." What do these words mean, and in your own words, what is Jesus claiming to be?

   _____
   _____
   _____

2. How is it different that Jesus says he *is* the truth as opposed to simply saying that he is preaching the truth?

3. Knowing Jesus is the truth, how might we use him then as an interpretive benchmark or standard for understanding not only the New Testament but also the Old Testament—everything in the Bible?

4. What do you think Jesus means by saying, "No one comes to the Father except through me"?

5. How might we apply these truths to being true followers of Jesus?

Further Study

1. As seen in Lesson 5, Jesus made quite a few bold claims concerning himself. Consider again these claims from the Gospel of John and what the implications are to following Jesus.
    a. I who speak to you am he [the Messiah], John 4:25–26.

    b. I am the bread of life, John 6:35, 48.

    c. I am the light of the world, John 8:12; 9:5.

    d. Before Abraham was, I am, John 8:58.

    e. I am the door, John 10:9.

    f. I am the good shepherd, John 10:11.

    g. I am the resurrection and the life, John 11:25.

    h. I am the true vine, John 15:1.

2. Read again John's purpose statement in John 20:30–31 for sharing the seven or eight miraculous signs he uses in his gospel. Do you believe that if the miracles, including Jesus's resurrection, are true that it is enough to cause you to follow him? Why or why not?

Key Scripture: Matthew 16:21–27—The call to follow.

1. Jesus called humankind to follow him because he is God. The cost of following him is the denial of our own rights to self-determination and to make the same sacrifice that he made. As the King of Kings, God tests each heart to determine if he will give that person a call to come to him. People do not come to Christ because they can't but because they won't. A person receives the call when the gospel is delivered to them, and they hear the invitation from God to come to his great feast. However, that person must then come humbly to God to be chosen by him. Jesus said, "For many are invited [called], but few are chosen." Many seemingly feel that coming to God is a right and a privilege. They often try to come to God for what they can get and feel no obligation as to what they owe him. The reality is God owes us nothing, and we owe him everything. Because of our curse of sin, we only deserve destruction; because of his great mercy, God offers us eternal life. If God's call has already come to you, how did it come?

2. As he was preparing the disciples to follow him, what did Jesus explain must happen to him when he went to Jerusalem, verse 21?

3. What was Peter's response to that, and why do you think he responded the way he did, verse 22?

4. What was Jesus's response to Peter, verse 23?

5. Why did Jesus say that Peter had come to the wrong conclusion, and how might an understanding of his mistake help us with our own follow-ship (discipleship) of Christ?

6. What did Jesus say the cost of any of our following him would be, verses 24–26?

7. In your own words, what does this mean to you—following Jesus in your own life?

8. Luke records this passage similarly, and in his version, he quotes Jesus as saying we would need to take up our cross "daily" (Luke 9:23). How does the insertion of "daily" into the text modify or amend the command?

9. Many, fearing a deadly Christian doctrine of "legalism," or "salvation by works," overreact to any mention of God rewarding works or deeds in any way. What does Jesus, however, say he will do for each of us when he returns, Matthew 16:27 (consider also his statements in Matt. 6:1–4)?

Further Study

1. In Luke 9:57–62, we are given three examples by Luke of individual encounters with Jesus. Consider what the issue and the subsequent cost is for each of them.
    a. "Foxes have dens and birds have nests, but the Son of Man has no place to lay his head" (Verses 57–58).

    b. "Let the dead bury their own dead, but you go and proclaim the kingdom of God" (Verses 59–60).

    c. "No one who puts a hand to the plow and looks back is fit for service in the kingdom of God" (Verses 60–62).

2. In an Old Testament story in 2 Chronicles 16:9, the prophet Hanani delivers a message to Asa, king of Judah, saying, "The eyes of the Lord range throughout the earth to strengthen those whose hearts are fully committed to him." At the root of discipleship is a heart that is fully committed to God. Do you think being fully committed to God means one is perfect, always strong, never feels doubt, and never sins? If not, what do you think it actually means?

Key Scripture: Luke 14:25–33—Counting the cost of following Jesus.

1. In some very hard and surprising language, Jesus lays out the real cost of following him. What is your initial response when you first read this text?

2. The Bible uses different kinds of literary devices and manners of speech to communicate, including idioms, jargons, slangs, and hyperboles. In this text, Jesus uses hyperbole in using the word "hate" to make the point that compared to our love for God, our affections for others may look more like hate. He also is likely using a type of Hebrew idiom such as was used in Genesis 29:30–31 with Jacob, Rachel, and Leah. It says Jacob loved Rachel but hated Leah, meaning his main allegiance was to Rachel not Leah. With that bit of explanation, what do you think Jesus is "getting at" in commanding us to hate those in our lives that are generally nearest and dearest to us?

3. Sometimes our decisions for God can cause great pain to those we love. Jesus's own decision to be persecuted, hated, and crucified is just such an example. Jesus's mother and brothers at one point came to take him home thinking he had "lost it" (Mark 3:31–32). He did not however go with them. In fact, he explained in verses 33–35 that it was those that obeyed God that were his true family, rather than simply his blood relatives. And in the end Mary had to endure seeing her son convicted for blasphemy and witness the unfair, hideous, torturous crucifixion he endured. He said he did not have to do it either. How might it be said that by letting such a brutal thing happen to himself that he had "hated" his mother and brothers?

4. What are the two metaphors in the main text above that Jesus uses to explain our need to count the cost of following him before we what might prove to be a hasty, embarrassing choice?

5. Why is it important for us to count the cost before we make the commitment to be a disciple? Consider Peter's strong warning in 2 Peter 2:20–22 concerning reversing one's decision to follow Christ?

6. What does it mean in verse 33 that it is necessary that we give up everything we have if we want to be a disciple?

Further Study

1. In Romans 12:1–2, Paul says that "in view of God's mercy," demonstrated by the cost of giving his own life for each of us, we should offer our own bodies as living sacrifices. List all the other things he commanded in this text and the resulting promise if we do so?

2. Read 2 Corinthians 5:14–15. Paul explains in this text what Christian service looks like.
   a. What does Paul say it is that should compel us as disciples?

   b. What does Christ want our response to be to his dying for us?

3. In Lesson 1, figure 1 we noted that major themes of the Old Testament and New Testament, respectively, might be said to be justice and mercy. It was further noted that these two great virtues of God combine at the crucifixion to fully express God's love. Jesus said some hard things during his ministry. Why do you suppose this kind of tough love, full of justice, yet full of mercy, is required to provoke each of us to fully pursue the way of Christ and to persevere in it?

Key Scripture: Luke 6:40—The reason to follow.

1. The goal of discipleship is not merely to *act like* Jesus; the goal is to *become like* him.
2. The translated Greek word "Christian" (*christianos*) is only used three times in the New Testament, in Acts 11:26; 26:28, and 1 Peter 4:16. Translators say the Greek word for "disciple" (*mathētēs*) is used 269 times! While the designation "Christian" has become quite generic and ill defined, the word "disciple" specifically means "a student, follower, or adherent." It is this specific definition that likely causes it to be most used, and it is also the lack of specificity that causes "Christian" not to be used much at all. "Disciple" was used to signify the kind of students who followed a rabbi, trying not only to learn faith from him, but also to imitate his life. Thus a student imitated his teacher. In the key scripture above, what did Jesus say the goal of a student or disciple is?

   _____
   _____
   _____

3. How does this differ from today's definition of a student?

   _____
   _____

4. The students of rabbis spent actual face time with the teacher, one on one and in a small group, learning from and imitating him in person. Since we cannot spend this same kind of time with Jesus in the flesh, what means did he give us to learn to imitate him?

   _____
   _____
   _____

Further Study

1. As considered earlier in 2 Corinthians 3:18, Paul discusses the impact that spending time with God had on Moses, as seen in the Old Testament, reminding us that Moses would become "radiant" (his face would somehow be aglow) after being with God. Moses would thus veil his face-to-keep from scaring the Israelites. Paul says that we will also radiate Christ as we spend time beholding him, and further that the Spirit will transform us to be more and more like him.
   a. How are we to "behold" or interact with the glory of Christ, as Moses did with God, in our present day?

      _____
      _____

   b. What do you suppose it "looks like" to radiate Christ's glory and goodness in our own lives?

      _____
      _____
      _____

2. The word used for "transform" is the word from which we get metamorphosis, which is the transformation process of a larva becoming an adult insect, such as a butterfly. Consider what this metamorphosis is to be in our lives as disciples.
   _____
   _____
   _____

3. Paul says that for him to live *is* Christ in Philippians 1:21. What does it mean to you to say, "to live *is* Christ"?
   _____
   _____
   _____

4. Paul also described the attitude of Christ that we should imitate in Philippians 2:5–8. In your own words, describe this attitude of Christ that we are to imitate.
   _____
   _____
   _____

5. What will that look like in the daily life of the disciple ("take up your cross daily")?
   _____
   _____
   _____

6. Further, in Philippians 3:7–14, Paul describes his own attitude. In your own words, how does Paul describe it?
   _____
   _____
   _____

Key Scripture: John 8:31–32—The way of following Christ.

1. Jesus points out that to be a genuine disciple one must "hold to his teachings." First of all, what do you suppose a disciple would look like who is not genuine?
   _____
   _____
   _____

2. What does it mean to "hold" to his teachings? Is this purely a mental thing as in believing it to be the truth, or do you think it is more than that? Explain.
   _____
   _____
   _____

3. Why do you think the concept of "knowing the truth" follows the idea of "holding to his teachings"?
   _____
   _____
   _____

4. Reading again in Romans 12:2, note that Paul says that when we offer our bodies as living sacrifices rather than being conformed to the pattern of the world (even the world's "Christian" pattern), we are transformed by renewing (resetting, changing, and correcting) our minds. What does he say being transformed will enable us to do, and how does it help us to "hold to Jesus's teaching"?

_____
_____
_____

Further Study

1. Jesus gives a new and all-encompassing command in John 13:34–35. All the Bible commands and instructions ultimately flow from it, and when they are obeyed with a good heart, they all flow from it. In fact, Jesus says doing this is how others can recognize that we are genuine disciples and not ones in pretension only, as we have seen discussed in other verses.
    a. What is this new command?

    _____
    _____
    _____

    b. Who and what are the standards by which we are to measure our obedience to this command?

    _____
    _____
    _____

2. Jesus uses a metaphor to emphasize the importance of being in him in John 15:1–8.
    a. Explain this metaphor in your own words.

    _____
    _____
    _____

    b. How much of his will does Jesus say we can get done on our own without his empowerment, verse 5?

    _____
    _____
    _____

    c. In this command, how does Jesus say that we show ourselves to be genuine disciples and what does this mean, verse 8?

    _____
    _____
    _____

Key Scripture: Matthew 4:19—The ministry and mission implication of following Jesus.

1. When we follow Jesus, there is not only a path we follow but also an identity and a purpose that we discover. What does Jesus say our purpose and identity become?

2. What do you think Jesus meant in saying that he would send those following him out to "fish for people"?

3. What method of fishing did his hearers likely use at that time?

4. How will understanding the difference between fishing with a net and our own idea of fishing with a line and a hook affect the way we "fish for people"?

5. Since this statement was to the original disciples, is there some reason to believe it does not apply to all disciples, given that we too are called to "follow him"?

6. How do you think that following Jesus down a life path of fishing for people and teaching them to also follow him will lead you to change your character and to take on a new identity?

Further Study

1. Read Mark 3:13–15. Here Mark tells about Jesus's appointing of the original twelve apostles. Why does Mark say Jesus appointed them?

2. Read Acts 8:1–4. What does Luke say all of the Christians did when they were driven out of Jerusalem?

    a. Do you believe Jesus appoints us similarly to preach and reach out to others? Why or why not?

    b. What do you think this should look like in each of our daily lives as disciples?

3. Read John 15:16. In this context, what is the fruit Jesus wants his people to bear for him?

Self-Reflection

1. Have I come to believe that Jesus truly is Lord?

2. How has studying this lesson affected my views on Jesus?

3. How has it affected my view of what my identity will be as a disciple?

4. Have I made the decision and commitment to be a genuine disciple?

5. If I have made that decision, why did I decide to do so?

6. If I have not, where am I in regard to making that decision?
   _____
   _____

7. What do I see as my strengths and weaknesses in regard to following Jesus?
   _____
   _____

8. What is the most important lesson or application of this lesson to my own life?
   _____
   _____

9. What one action will I purpose to take in moving forward?
   _____
   _____
   _____

LESSON 8

Accepting Christ as Your Savior: Faith, Repentance, and Baptism

INTRODUCTION

ODDLY ENOUGH, WHAT OUGHT TO be one of the simplest parts of being a Christian—becoming one—can be one of the most confusing parts. There is quite a debate that has long raged among churches regarding the requirements for becoming a Christian. This is partly because countless individuals, churches, organizations, and cultures have contributed for over two thousand years to an ongoing development of Christian belief and practice. Furthermore, the inevitable dissensions that occur among fallen humans have both complicated and enriched that development (1 Cor. 11:19). Overreactions of one group to another along the way have fixated some denominations and groups on certain principles or doctrines to the neglect of others. In trying to address certain beliefs that were considered wrong, overcorrections in the other direction have occurred. The scriptures themselves at times seem to confirm and reject these fixations depending on what is emphasized. However, reading the scripture in its totality and according to its own authority will help us resolve *some* of these complicated issues. More importantly, learning to trust the God that scripture declares emphatically is in control rather than trying to control things ourselves will lead us to trust. Trust will lead us to truth. And Jesus is the truth.

The most important thing for us to understand, and the one principle that underlies all others, is that one must come to an unequivocal and deeply abiding faith in God. Our chief responsibility is to simply trust God. The gospel at its core is the revelation about the true identity and nature of God—he is just and good! His love is immeasurable, his mercy unimaginable, his godly nature immutable, and his patience incomparable. His power is infinite, his knowledge and wisdom incomprehensible, his purposes undefeatable, and his presence undeniable. These attributes as well as his innumerable others are clearly beheld in the things that he made so that unbelief is inexcusable (Psa. 14:1; Rom. 1:20). The ultimate good news to us is that this awesome God deeply desires a relationship with us as honest seekers and that he actually seeks us out (2 Chron. 16:9; John 4:23–24). Salvation is by grace—the incredible grace of God that is extended to us through our willingness to put our trust in Christ.

This lesson will examine the scriptures about how one should respond to the gospel call and come into a right relationship with God.

Key Scripture: Mark 1:15—Repenting And Believing The Good News Of The Kingdom Of God.

1. The religious mind-set of Jesus's primary audience in Israel was somewhat unique within itself. Israel was diverse enough in terms of beliefs and practices, but at the time of Jesus, there was still a strong

sentiment about being once more a great country, as it was during the time of King David. So national fervor was intense among some, religious fervor of various nuances was strong among others, and the influences of Greco-Roman culture were all around as well. How do you think the storyline would go if Jesus were to come to modern America? Think for a moment about how he would be received, how different groups would react to him, how the government and established religions would interact with him, how various church groups might respond, how he would impact the "sinners," and what his impact would be on the social outcasts and marginalized of our culture. Write down a few thoughts to gain a better visual.

a. To the ancient Jews of the Old Testament, a relationship with God was likely seen as more a birthright of sorts than anything else. What similarity do you see with Christianity and modern America as well as religious views of most countries?

b. Pleasing God was about obeying Torah—the Law of Moses. As with most religions, great concern was given to those practices others could observe—Sabbath observance, obeying the food laws, observing various festivals and such, and so forth. Why do you think religious people focus on the outside—what others can see—more than they focus on the inner person?

c. The apostle Paul recognized this as a futile attempt by fallen men to attain or earn salvation and that it was an impossible feat, even though he himself was a law keeper (Gal. 3–5; Rom 7; Phil. 3:6). How do you think you have tried to earn your own place with God, or how have you seen it in others—particularly among Christians and other religious people you might know?

d. The Law is in fact clearly a manifestation of the Tree of the Knowledge of Good and Evil from the Garden of Eden. It revealed the "knowledge of good and knowledge of evil." And just like the forbidden tree fruit, although the knowledge the Law gave was good and true, no human could be right with God through it. Attempts at law keeping will bring death to those who eat of it (Gal. 3:10–13). Having and keeping a unique law represented then, and still represents, humanity's desire for self-reliance and control in "saving itself" and being "like God, by knowing good and evil" (Gen. 3:1–7). Why do we yearn so much for control, self-determination, and self-reliance?

e. The Law was perfect and good, but it only revealed that humanity was not, and therefore the Law, or law keeping, could not save us (Rom. 7:9–13; Gal. 3:21). Why could the Law then not bring salvation to those who sought to keep it?

_____
_____

f. Oddly, in trying to obey the Law—any religious law, in fact—most people seemingly are ultimately drawn away from God rather than to him. The whole nation of Israel can be seen as drawing away from God over and over in their quest to build their own earthly kingdom out of Israel rather than letting God be their king (1 Sam. 8:6–9). When we clearly are very limited in our own powers over even our own lives, let alone the rest of this expansive universe, why do you suppose it is our human nature to need to be self-reliant and self-determined?

_____
_____

g. When through Jesus God actually came to Israel to be their king, they rejected God again, as they had done over and over in their history (John 1:10–11). Why do you think humankind rejects God's merciful and powerful divine guidance and oversight, opting rather to attempt to rely on our own weak and piteous selves, and what does that tell you about humankind's prevailing views of ourselves and our often prevailing views of God?

_____
_____

2. There are four important concepts mentioned in Jesus's simple statement in Mark 1:15—the kingdom of God, repentance, belief, and the "good news" (gospel). Consider the four:
   a. The kingdom of God. Strangely, although the idea of a kingdom itself is easily grasped, the idea of a kingdom of God is not so much so. Answer briefly why you think this is so, and then consider the statements that follow.

   _____
   _____

      i. Jesus has all authority in heaven and on earth (Matt. 28:18)—therefore, he is king.
      ii. The word "Christ" literally means "the anointed one" or "king." It is not a part of his name, but it is his title or position.
      iii. Jesus only accepts into his kingdom those who hear his call and willingly surrender to his kingship. If one's heart is not acceptable to God, he or she cannot surrender to God, (John 6:44; Matt. 22:11–12).
      iv. It is essential then that we strive to get our hearts in the right attitude before God—humble, thankful, and so forth. God sees our thoughts and feelings as behavior (Jer. 17:9–10).
      v. Jesus said his kingdom is not something that is observable or visible but rather something within and among us (Luke 17:20–21).
      vi. Israel was never the kingdom of God, but only a "type" (foreshadowing) of the "antitype" (the reality), which was to come.

vii. Jesus was officially coroneted by God after his death and burial, and after God had thus raised him from the dead (Phil. 2:5–11).
viii. The kingdom is spoken of in future tense (Matt. 6:10) all the way up to that Pentecost Sunday in Jerusalem (Acts 2), when the Holy Spirit was poured out and three thousand people surrendered to Christ's Lordship (Acts 2:36–40).
ix. After this event, the kingdom is spoken of in past tense, as having already been established (Col. 1:13; Rev. 1:9).
x. The kingdom is clearly still under construction (John 14:1–4). What do you think the "kingdom of God" is, and why is it near when Christ is near?

_____
_____
_____

b. Repentance. Consider the following.
   i. The word "repentance" means "to change your mind."
   ii. In order to believe (to trust God), one will have to change his or her mind from not believing in the mercy and goodness of God to believing it—to move from self-reliance to God-reliance.
   iii. Belief in God is first a decision based on the evidence, and then it takes both mind *and* heart effort to believe it (Heb. 11:1; John 6:29; Matt. 22:37).
   iv. Repentance will always be evidenced in one's behavior. If behavior does not change accordingly, repentance never really occurred (2 Cor. 7:10–11; Matt. 21:28–32).
   v. Why do you think it takes a drastic change of mind and heart to truly believe the good news of Christ?

_____
_____
_____

c. Belief.
   i. In scripture, the exact meaning of the word "believe" or "belief" must be determined by how it is used in each context. Various words in all languages must be defined by their contexts. Other words often used synonymously with belief are "faith," "confidence," "trust," and "hope."
   ii. There are three facets or degrees of a "saving belief" (not all belief is saving belief), as seen in scripture, and the text itself will reveal which facet or degree is being implied. We have to be careful because the word "belief" may indicate any one of, or all, of these facets or degrees. They are below:
      1) A *mental ascent* to a certain truth. But even demons have this, and they certainly are not saved (James 2:19).
      2) *Acceptance of* or *surrendering to* the truth. One can certainly know something and disregard it completely.
      3) Living *a life* or having *a lifestyle* in accordance with the truth. With regularity any one of us might live and behave inconsistently with what we believe. The scripture says that the righteous will "live by faith," and if they turn back from it, God will not be pleased with them (Heb. 10:38). Paul says to believe and then to turn back is to "believe in vain" (1 Cor. 15:2).

4) Why do you suppose a "saving faith" (one that pleases and satisfies God) requires all three facets or degrees to be complete in God's eyes?
___
___
___

5) Compare our faith relationships in marriage to our faith relationships to God:
   a. When we meet and get to know someone we believe might be the right person for us, what degree of faith does that compare to?
   ___
   ___
   ___

   b. When we make the commitment, get engaged, and go through the marriage ceremony, what level of faith does this compare to?
   ___
   ___

   c. When we have lived long and full lives as faithful mates to the one we originally vowed our love and devotion to, what degree of faith does that compare to?
   ___
   ___

   d. Only when facing death could the apostle Paul say that he had "kept the faith" (2 Tim. 4:7). Jesus said that if we would be faithful to death, he would give us our crown of life (Rev. 2:10). Paul said that if we were to ever shrink back from our faith, whatever belief we had possessed would have been in vain (1 Cor. 15:2). Why do you suppose this is so, and how does this compare to being a faithful mate?
   ___
   ___
   ___

d. The gospel is what we must believe in order to be saved and to become a part of Christ's kingdom.
   i. It is our faith in the gospel that pleases God, changes our hearts and lives, and brings us into his eternal kingdom. We come to trust him—his love, his mercy, his goodness, his supremacy, his wisdom, his way, and so forth—rather than ourselves.
   ii. What *is* the gospel?
       1) Many see it merely as what Jesus *did* for us in his death, burial, and resurrection to atone for our sins, and certainly that *is* the pinnacle of gift to us.
       2) But the gospel is not ultimately about *what God did* for us through his death on the cross; the gospel is about *the glorious nature of God* that caused him to die for us in the first place. The good news is about who our creator is!

3) God is an awesome, wonderful, loving, merciful, powerful, long-suffering, brilliant, creative heavenly Father who wants an eternal relationship with each of us. Why is that such good news?

_____
_____
_____

4) To be with God is to be with everything that is good. And that is great news for those who come to understand it and accept him by faith. The bad news is that the opposite is true of those who choose not to surrender to him. They will ultimately live eternally without all that is good.

5) Based on all that you have seen so far about who God is, write out your own best description of how you see God himself, his love and mercy for you through the gospel of Christ, and his desire for you to come to him.

_____
_____
_____

Further Study

1. Read Romans 1:16–17. Some have described Paul's letter to the Roman church as the "gospel according to Paul."
   a. In Paul's letter to Romans, he writes a veritable commentary about the meaning and application of the gospel of Christ in our lives.
      i. In this passage, Paul says he is not ashamed of the gospel because it represents the truth about God that can save us. What, however, might cause one to be ashamed of the gospel?

      _____
      _____

      ii. The choice of believing the gospel or not believing the gospel still comes down to the choices represented by the two trees in the Garden of Eden—the Tree of the Knowledge of Good and Evil and the Tree of Life.
      iii. As has repeatedly been noted in this study, the former represents an attempt at achieving our own righteousness through knowledge of what is right and being able to live it out exactly.
      iv. The latter represents what Paul is writing about—the "righteousness that comes from God and is by faith from first to last." In the latter, rather than God seeing us as "righteous" by our own merit (which clearly is unattainable for us), God sees us as righteous through his own loving, merciful eyes (Eph. 1:4; Rom. 8:1–4).
      v. Consider how "self-righteousness" is all about having faith in ourselves—as if to say, "I can do it myself!" Which in this case, we clearly cannot, and are in fact utter failures when we try!

Righteousness achieved is opposite of the righteousness that is given to us by God. Why is self-righteousness completely contrary to having faith in God?

_____
_____
_____

2. Read Romans 7:6. Paul says that through Christ things had changed from Jewish attempts at living by Law to a completely new way—a way of faith.
   a. Because of what Christ did, we now serve in the "new way of the Spirit, not in the old way of the written code." What does it mean to attempt to have the life of God through living by a written code (law)?

   _____
   _____
   _____

   b. Paul also says that when Christ died on the cross, he nailed the written code to the cross, disarming the power of Satan to accuse us by our violations of the Law (Col. 2:13–15; James 2:10). How is this so?

   _____
   _____
   _____

   c. Consider why trying to live and have a relationship with God, and each other for that matter, according to the written code requires trusting in self and why living by the Spirit requires trusting in God.

   _____
   _____
   _____

Key Scripture: John 3:1–5—Being born again.

1. Jesus described our salvation as a rebirth—as being born again.
2. Nicodemus, the one talking to Jesus, was a part of the Sanhedrin.
   a. The Sanhedrin served with the high priest as the highest ruling body in Israel, although Israel was of course under the ultimate rule of the Roman Empire.
   b. Nicodemus probably came to Jesus under the cover of night because Jesus had already fallen out of favor with the Jewish leaders at large.
      i. Thus being seen meeting with Jesus would cause problems.
      ii. He seems to be trying to figure this "Jesus person" out for himself and begins with a compliment, perhaps implying his question.
      iii. After reading the account, why do you think he was approaching Jesus, and why did he start the conversation the way he did?

      _____
      _____
      _____

3. Jesus's first reply in verse 3 may seem a little rude. What did Jesus say to him and why do you think he said it?

4. Nicodemus seems to bristle just a bit and is perhaps cynical in his own follow-up question in verse 4. What does he say?

5. Jesus then further expounds a bit on his first answer in verse 5. What is his answer to Nicodemus?

6. What does Jesus say must happen for one to enter the kingdom of God, and what do you think this means?

7. Compare John 3:3–5; Romans 6:3–11; Matthew 3:13–17; and Acts 2:38. (Also, look at John 3:22–23 and 4:1–2 to see what John begins to tell about right after he tells Nicodemus's story.) It seems clear based on Paul's explanation of baptism, the example of Jesus's baptism, and the promise concerning baptism from Peter on Pentecost that Jesus was talking about the baptism that Peter instituted when the church was first established (Acts 2). Do you agree or disagree?

8. Given the strong statements of the New Testament about the mode and meaning of baptism, why do you suppose many churches and Christians have rejected the act of water baptism as having any relationship to our salvation, opting rather to believe it is accomplished through an acceptance prayer, a form actually never seen in scripture as the pattern of the New Testament church?

Further Study

1. Read Romans 6:3–11 and list everything Paul says happens to us in baptism.

2. Read Acts 2:38–39 and relate what Peter commands and promises to what Jesus said about rebirth.

3. Read 1 Corinthians 12:13 and relate this statement with what Jesus said about rebirth.

Key Scripture: Acts 16:30–32—Being saved.

1. If you have previous Christian experience, how have you defined "being saved," or otherwise, how have you heard it described?

2. Briefly summarize Acts 16:30–32.

3. Notice the situation.
    a. The jailer in this story was a Roman official who probably had no previous experience with the true God of Israel, nor had he likely ever heard much if anything at all about Jesus. As did most Romans, he likely believed in many gods.
    b. He had probably been involved in the unjust flogging of Paul and Silas (Acts 16:16–24) and then chaining them to the jail wall so they could find no comfort.
    c. Sometime after midnight, during their worshiping, an earthquake freed them from their chains and opened the prison doors. However, almost as miraculously, not a single prisoner left!
    d. Given the miraculous event, why do you suppose the jailer was then about to kill himself?

    e. What do you think the jailer was really asking when he asked the question, "What must I do to be saved," since he likely had no concept of salvation through Christ? That is, what was this jailer's main concern at this point?

    f. What was Paul's answer to him?

g. Given what you have learned to this point, why do you suppose belief in Jesus must be the foundation of our response to Christ?

_____
_____

h. To explain, the jailer most likely was not asking a theological or doctrinal question about salvation, but one about his own survival. This was due to the fact that the God of Paul and Silas had just miraculously freed them with an earthquake. Yet no prisoners tried to escape. But even though the jailor likely had mere survival on his mind, the answer still deals with ultimate meaning of salvation. What is it that the Savior Jesus Christ offers to us, and what then does it mean to you "to be saved"?

_____
_____

4. The expressions "being or getting saved," "being forgiven," "being born again," "becoming a Christian," and so forth all refer basically to the same thing—being forgiven by God and coming into a right relationship with him by God's own will and grace, and through the work of the Holy Spirit (1 Cor. 12:13). What have been your own personal, denominational, or traditional views of how salvation comes to pass in one's life?

_____
_____
_____

5. Where did your views originate and why?

_____
_____

6. Why is it paramount for all disciples to clearly determine in their own minds what God's actual commands are for our coming to him?

_____
_____
_____

Further Study

1. Read 1 Timothy 1:15. This is a statement the apostle Paul makes in one of his letters concerning his own salvation.
    1. Most of the time when we are seeking favor with another, especially favor completely undeserved, we paint ourselves in the best possible light so as to seem somehow worthy of the favor. Children learn how to do this very quickly. What did Paul however do in this regard, as seen in this verse?

    _____
    _____
    _____

2. How did Paul see himself in terms of his worthiness to receive salvation?

2. Read the following verses that specifically mention "being saved," and consider what each has to say.
   1. Ephesians 2:8–9

   2. Acts 2:38–40

   3. Acts 16:29–34

   4. Romans 10:9, 10, 13

   5. Mark 16:15–16

Key Scripture: Hebrew 11:1, 6—The essentiality of faith.

1. The kind of faith God requires is not blind, as some would claim it to be, but in fact is confident and sure. And it is essential in order to have a relationship with God. How is true faith in God based on reason and evidence, as opposed to the kind of blind faith that depends on personal preference, feelings, heritage, and so forth?

2. How does the Bible define faith in verse 1?

3. What does it mean to have confidence and assurance concerning God, or anything else for that matter?

4. Why do you suppose the components mentioned here are essential to the kind of faith that will bring us into a right relationship with God?

5. Why do you think that it is impossible to please God unless you have faith in him?

Further Study

1. As previously mentioned, the words "faith," "belief," "confidence," "hope," "conviction," and "trust" are sometimes used synonymously or somewhat synonymously in scripture.
    a. As a family of words, they describe a state of being persuaded about the truth or validity of something, and specifically in the Bible about believing in God and his son Jesus Christ.
    b. The precise meaning that is being communicated in a text must be determined by the context.
    c. Sadly, like most things having to do with religion, the contextual meanings of these words are sometimes debated. The roots of these debates, and thus the intensity of them, are rooted in centuries of church traditions.
    d. But salvation is found in a simple faith that God is in control, not us, not our church, and not our culture. He understands that compared to him we are weak and all too finite, and thus our salvation is not contingent on our perfection in anything, including our faith and understanding of God.
    e. Our salvation rests on the reality that God that is willing to forgive us and to give us a hope that we can be with him forever, and all of this based on his goodness not our own.
    f. Our salvation rests on our trust in God—on the belief that his death on the cross tells us about an incredibly graceful, forgiving God who himself has paid the ultimate price for our sin. He died in the place of each of us. How should this reality make us feel toward God?

    g. Our very existence is a gift of God. Our faith is a gift of God. And our hope rests on God. Remember, biblical hope means our expectation of good to come. How does our faith produce hope within us?

h. When we allow ourselves to be bound up in intense and fruitless debates about where faith comes from, about what exactly constitutes faith, about who has enough faith or too little, and at what point our faith brings salvation, we risk entering into a realm that is not about faith in God at all but rather is about faith in ourselves, our reasoning, our rightness, our traditions, our belief systems, our church heroes, and so forth. Faith at its purest is about a "pure and sincere devotion to Christ" (2 Cor. 11:3). What things do you see that can in fact interfere with a simple, pure devotion to Christ?

i. Faith is surrender, not conquest. Faith is submission, not control. Faith is confidence in God, not confidence in self. Faith frees us, not enslaves us. Faith causes us to feel indebted, not entitled.

j. How do you think getting caught up in religious arguments about faith can actually be counter to faith and thus hinder our salvation and walk with God?

2. As already mentioned, a saving faith in the gospel has three essential elements. In 1 Corinthians 15:1–2, Paul reminds the Corinthian converts of their own conversions. In it he uses three descriptions of their responses to Christ. Each of them refers to a facet of what might be seen as a saving faith, as opposed to the kind of "faith" even a demon has (James 2:19). These principles can be seen in *Vine's Dictionary of New Testament Words* under the definition of the word "faith." Consider carefully that faith as described here is from "first to last," from beginning to end, and requires the faith to be "kept" (Rom. 1:16–17; 2 Tim. 4:7).

   a. *You received the gospel* = an acceptance of the truth. What does it mean to accept something as being true?

   b. *You took your stand on the gospel* = a surrender to the truth. What does it mean to take a stand on something or surrender to a call to something?

   c. *You are saved by the gospel if you hold firmly to the end, otherwise you have believed in vain* = a life inspired by surrender. What does it mean to hold firmly to something you believe and have taken a stand on?

   d. What does it mean to believe something in vain?

3. Read the following scriptures and consider what each has to say about faith or belief.
   a. John 3:16–17

   b. Ephesians 2:8–9

   c. Mark 9:24

   d. Romans 1:16–17

   e. Romans 5:1–2

Key Scripture: Acts 2:1–47—Repentance is faith's point of decision.

1. Please take the time to read this whole text before continuing.
2. In Acts 1:1–5, we read about Jesus's work with the apostles after his resurrection. Luke tells the story of the forty plus days that Jesus spent with the apostles after his resurrection teaching them about the kingdom of God, promising them the coming of the Holy Spirit, and reiterating their mission of taking the gospel to the world.
3. The outpouring of the Holy Spirit came as promised by Jesus. In the first part of Acts 2, the Holy Spirit is shown being poured out for all people. John the Baptist had promised that Jesus would baptize with the Holy Spirit (Mark 1:8), and Luke records Christ as having done so shortly after his return to heaven.
4. In Acts 2:14–40, we have recorded the first account of believers being saved.
   a. The scene would clearly, in our present-day context, look more like a lively evangelistic revival than it would an everyday church service. It was certainly a one-of-a-kind event. Is the Holy Spirit's direct action always expected to be ecstatic, emotional, or even appear supernatural? Give your reasoning.

b. The apostles of Christ, who were the foundation of the church, led this exchange between the apostles and the Jews gathered, with Peter as the spokesman. Luke, a skilled historian, gives a brief but careful account of this evangelistic meeting. Briefly write a synopsis about the key things that happened that day.

_____
_____

c. This is the first time the full gospel had been preached, and some of these would become the first converts.

d. This is an important foundational example of unbelievers becoming believers, non-Christians becoming Christians, unsaved becoming saved, unforgiven being forgiven, and so forth.

e. Note in verses 22, 23, and 36 how Peter summarizes the Jews' treatment of Jesus.

_____
_____

5. What is the noted response of many of them to Peter's accusation against them and the question they asked in response, verse 37?

_____
_____

6. What is the first thing, upon their coming to believe, that Peter tells them to do, and why? (Belief of course is being implied but is not specifically mentioned here.)

_____
_____

7. As previously mentioned, repentance means to change your mind. How did the audience need to change their minds, and what specifically did they need to repent of?

_____
_____

8. In reading Acts 2:40–47, how can it be seen that their behavior and lifestyle changes indicate their true repentance?

_____
_____
_____

Further Study

1. Read 2 Corinthians 7:10–11. What two kinds of sorrows are mentioned here? Compare and contrast them in your own words.

_____
_____
_____

2. Which of these two leads to repentance?

3. How can we be sure that repentance has occurred in ourselves or in others around us?

4. Consider each of the words Paul uses to describe the fruit of genuine repentance. This is an individualized exchange with one certain church, thus, the words used are specific to what he saw as the necessary responses they needed to adopt at that time. However, the ideas reflected here are important aspects of what the Bible calls true repentance. This can as well be seen through other scriptures. What do you think each of these means in terms of Bible definitions? Use a commentary or Bible dictionary to look them up if you can.

   a. Earnestness

   b. Eagerness to clear yourselves

   c. Indignation

   d. Alarm

   e. Longing

   f. Concern

   g. Readiness to see justice done

5. Read Matthew 21:28–32, which is a parable Jesus spoke about a father and his two sons. Although in many translations the word "repent" is not used, the parable illustrates what repentance is. In the parable, a father gives his two sons a command to go work in the vineyards. One said he was going to obey but did not. The other said he would not but then changed his mind (repented) and obeyed his father.
   a. Consider the context of this parable. Whom was Jesus pointing out as being like the first son, and whom was Jesus pointing out as being like the second son?

   _____
   _____
   _____

   b. How might this be applied today, especially to the biblical concept of repentance?

   _____
   _____
   _____
   _____

Key Scripture: Romans 6:1–14—Baptism is the simple method or rite God gave us for accepting Christ by faith.

1. Romans is a letter Paul wrote in which he explains the salvation that God offers humanity by his own grace expressed through his redeeming work at the cross. In his letter, after explaining the concept of salvation by grace through faith, he deals with an obvious question that will arise when one sees their salvation solely as a freely given gift of God.
   a. A key question is, "Does grace mean we can just commit whatever sins we want and God will just forgive it no matter what?" The answer is not simple, but in the context of this question Paul explains the significance and meaning of baptism in our conversions.
   b. Obviously, the original recipients already had some prior knowledge about all of this through their own conversions, and Paul surely assumes conversion as something that has already happened in any Christian.
   c. He nonetheless explains what God does for us in this act of baptism that he has given us.
   d. Unlike other commands God gives us, baptism is something done *to* us not *by* us.
   e. The act of being baptized by another person is an outward expression of an inward reality, a rebirth that is accomplished on the inside of us by the Holy Spirit through baptism. Note that while baptism is indeed symbolic, the scripture assigns actual meanings to it and not just symbolism.
   f. Beginning in verse 3 of the text, notice all that the apostle Paul says God does in our receiving Christ this way. He never says or even infers that baptism is only symbolic, although no one should doubt it is full of symbolism. Make a note what each means to you.
   g. Baptized into Christ Jesus:

   _____
   _____
   _____

   h. Baptized into his death:

   _____
   _____
   _____

i. Buried with him in baptism:

j. Raised with him in baptism:

k. To have a new life:

l. Old self was crucified with him:

m. No longer slaves to sin:

n. Freed from sin:

o. Will live with Christ:

p. Count selves alive to God and dead to sin:

2. Many have naturally compared baptism in the New Testament to circumcision in the Old Testament, and concluded it is a "work" that is only symbolic and is not something involved in salvation. However, baptism is not actually a work of ours at all, unless of course one believes it merits salvation in some way. Baptism is an act of faith. Consider and briefly summarize these scriptures.
   a. Paul says that in baptism that we are "raised with him through our faith in the working of God" (Col. 2:12). Our faith must never be in ourselves. Our faith must be in the "working of God." Why do you think this is so?

b. Paul explains the natural connection of our faith to our baptism as a progression and not two different things (Gal. 3:26–27). Baptism is simply the way God has given us to accept Christ as our Savior and Lord.

c. Peter calls our baptism "the pledge of a clear conscience toward God" saying in fact that "baptism… now saves you" (1 Pet. 3:21).

d. Peter says we are baptized for the forgiveness of sins with the promise of receiving the Holy Spirit (Acts 2:38–39).

e. By Paul's own account, Ananias told Paul to be baptized to "wash away his sins" (Acts 22:16).

Further Study

1. Read John 9:1–7 about a blind man Jesus healed.
    a. Notice that although Jesus could have simply cured this man's blindness with a spoken word, he did not. He actually did something that to us seems gross; he made mud with his own saliva and rubbed it in the man's eyes. Then he told him to go wash in a certain pool.
    b. I doubt there are many that would suggest that the mud or the water of the pool cured this man's blindness. Clearly God healed the blindness.
    c. Jesus did it because of the man's faith, the faith that was manifested and expressed by the blind man's simple, trusting obedience. No one would suggest that the man's actions in any way earned him healing. It was his trust that allowed him to be healed. It is the same with us as Christians. If God says to do a thing for such and such reason, why do we have to figure out what and how God is doing what he does through it? Why can't we just trust him and do what he says?

    d. Who can doubt that if the man had failed to simply obey Jesus by faith that he likely would not have been cured?
    e. What do you think are the key points of this particular miracle of Christ?

f. Baptism and the Lord's Supper are two rites that God has asked us to receive that seem to have significant meaning to him, and through which he determined to act on behalf of those who obeyed him. As with baptism, the Lord's Supper is certainly rich in symbolism, hearkening all the way back to the Passover festival of Israel. However, even with the symbolism, Jesus said the bread *is* his body and the cup *is* his blood. Jesus said he would be with us in it. Why is it sometimes so hard for us to believe that God acts through our actions, such as he does in prayer and worship?

_____
_____
_____

g. Why do you suppose God might use certain actions or rites to test our faith, when after all, he already knows and sees our faith before we do anything?

_____
_____
_____

2. In the Book of Acts, Luke gives us several accounts of various conversions. The first notable thing about these is how extraordinarily different they are from each other. We humans like to package things neatly and consistently. However, God's ways are not our ways, and each of these demonstrates the direct action of God. A second notable part of these accounts is that the only thing all of these conversion stories have in common is that they all end with baptism—water baptism. Read each of the conversion stories, noting how each person or group received Christ. Notice the things mentioned about what they were told and commanded and what their specific responses were. Note their differences and their similarities. What are your own thoughts and conclusions from each of these examples?

   a. Acts 2:38–41—Jews at Pentecost

   _____
   _____
   _____

   b. Acts 8:12–13—Samaritans

   _____
   _____
   _____

   c. Acts 8:26–39—Ethiopian man

   _____
   _____
   _____

   d. Acts 9:1–9 (Acts 22:3–16)—Conversion of Saul/Apostle Paul

   _____
   _____
   _____

   e. Acts 10:44–48—Cornelius and household

   _____
   _____
   _____

    f. Acts 16:13–15—Lydia and household

    g. Acts 16:25–34—Roman jailer

    h. Acts 18:7–8—Corinthians

    i. Acts 19:1–7—Ephesians

3. In addition to the consideration of the meaning and purpose of water baptism is the question of the intended mode or form.
    a. Is biblical baptism in the form of immersion, pouring, or sprinkling? Do you think this matters to God? Write a note to explain your logic.

    b. This is a debatable topic—one the church has disagreed on over the centuries.
    c. One's view of baptism depends on one's approach to scripture and church, as well as one's view of God.
        i. Many believe in following exact patterns set out in the Bible through stories and examples.
        ii. Others believe in "freedom of forms" in regard to the various ways Christians respond to God.
        iii. The opinion here is that immersion is still the biblically desirable form, since the Greek word used in scripture meant to "immerse." There were other words for sprinkling water and pouring water.
        iv. A further reason for supporting immersion is that baptism is meant to symbolize a death, burial, and resurrection, something well symbolized by immersion but not so much in sprinkling or pouring.
    d. However, the important thing is *not* that one knows and understands everything about God's purposes and ways, because that is not even possible (Isa. 55:9). Paul said it this way, "Oh, the depth of the riches of the wisdom and knowledge of God! How unsearchable his judgments, and his paths beyond tracing out!" (Rom. 11:33). Rephrase Paul's statement in your own simpler words.

    e. In reality the important thing is not even that one has a *great heart* or a *great faith*.
    f. The important thing is that one has *a sincere heart and an honest faith*! We need to believe that God really loves and wants a relationship with us. We need to sincerely believe that he has paid the price for our salvation—a price we could never pay ourselves.

g. The reality is that in principle no "correct" rite or ritual can erase a bad, dishonest heart, and likely no "incorrect" rite or ritual will ever disqualify an honest, sincere heart from a right relationship with a merciful God. Why do you agree or disagree?

h. Humble submission in coming to him as we are, is what is required. Arguably it is better to do the wrong thing the wrong way but with the right heart than to do the right thing the right way but with a wrong heart!

i. Summarize your own feelings concerning the meaning of water baptism.

j. Summarize your own thoughts and opinions on the method or mode of baptism.

Key Scripture: Titus 3:3–7—The "washing of rebirth and renewal by the Holy Spirit."

1. Our salvation is described by the apostle Paul as a "washing of rebirth and renewal by the Holy Spirit." Describe in your own words the positive definitions of the key words used in this verse.
    a. Washing:

    b. Rebirth:

    c. Renewal:

    d. Holy Spirit:

2. How do these verses relate to what we have studied about the roles of faith, repentance, and baptism in our rebirths when we receive Christ as Lord and Savior?

3. Paul summarizes the idea of conversion. How does he describe us before conversion, verse 3?
   _____
   _____
   _____

4. How does he describe God's nature and actions in our conversions, verses 4–5?
   _____
   _____
   _____

5. How does he describe our being saved, verses 5–7?
   _____
   _____
   _____

Self-Reflection

1. Have I ever truly accepted Christ as my Savior? Describe.
   _____
   _____
   _____

2. Did I believe I also accepted him as my Lord? Describe.
   _____
   _____
   _____

3. How might accepting Jesus personally as my Savior and accepting him personally as my Lord differ?
   _____
   _____

4. What are my best takeaways from this lesson that I want to apply in my own life (go back and review the various scriptures and points, along with notes you may have written)?
   _____
   _____
   _____

5. What questions do I have, or what was confusing to me?
   _____
   _____
   _____

6. Are there things I need to do in regard to my own relationship with God?
   _____
   _____
   _____

7. How has my heart been toward God, and how might that need to change or improve?

8. Do I need to take the step of accepting Christ as Lord and Savior and obeying him in repentance and baptism? Briefly explain the reasoning.

9. Who do I know that might be able to help me start a relationship with Christ, if I do not already have one?

10. As a Christian, whom do I know that might be able to help me grow spiritually?

11. Whom might I know that I can help come to accept Christ or otherwise to grow in their relationship with him?

LESSON 9

Living by the Holy Spirit

§

INTRODUCTION

THE NEW TESTAMENT TEACHES US how to live by the Spirit. The Old Testament is a story about the death that results from our choosing self-reliance over reliance on God, that is, when we choose the Tree of the Knowledge of Good and Evil over the Tree of Life. The new way of Christ is the new way of the Spirit (Rom. 7:6). Although the Spirit was active from the beginning in the creation itself, he apparently only acted in and around specific people and in specific ways, not easily accessible to everyone. However, the Old Testament prophet promised that the Holy Spirit would one day be "poured out on all flesh" (Joel 2:28–29). John the Baptist announced the Spirit's impending coming and that it was Jesus who would send him (Matt. 3:11). Paul said the Sons of God were those who were led by the Holy Spirit of God (Rom. 8:14).

On the Pentecost, when Peter first preached the full gospel of Christ, he made a promise on behalf of God that those who repented and were baptized would receive the "gift of the Holy Spirit," saying, "The promise is for you and your children and for all who are far off—for all whom the Lord our God will call" (Acts 2:39). The Holy Spirit is to the Book of Acts what Jesus is to the four gospels; the Spirit is the main character. Acts then is the story of how the church began and spread from Jerusalem to the center of the Roman Empire, which was in Rome, all by the power and work of the Holy Spirit through Christ's church.

Learning to live by the Holy Spirit is ultimately the most critical lesson of all for a Christian. Receiving God in this way is the great promise of the New Covenant—"And you will receive the gift of the Holy Spirit" (Acts 2:38). For various reasons there are some confusing and sometimes even frightening ideas circulating about the Holy Spirit's work among Christians and in churches, but in the end, his work should not be frightening to us. Rather, it should produce within us the greatest hope of all—the expectation of Christ working in us to accomplish his redemptive work in us and those we touch (Col. 1:27)!

There is no single passage that gives a definitive, complete description of God's Holy Spirit. As already noted, he is simply mentioned as working throughout the scriptures from beginning to end. Similarly, the Holy Spirit is still at work in and around us today in a variety of ways. The Greek word for spirit is *pneuma*. It is generally translated "spirit, wind, or breath," depending on the context. Jesus himself compared the work of the Spirit in our lives to the forces of wind on earth (John 3:5–8), explaining that you could not see where the wind comes from or where it is going, but only that it is present through its effects.

Thus a working understanding and appreciation of the person and work of the Holy Spirit of God must be built from what might be called a scriptural "construct." (A "construct" or "hypothetical construct" in psychological or scientific theory explains a phenomenon, that is not directly observable, by identifying observable effects of that phenomenon.) Therefore, although we may not be able to observe directly the comings and goings of the Holy Spirit, we can however come to know about how he works through various available scriptures. We can in our mind's eye visualize the effects of his work from the many stories and descriptions of his nature and his activities the Bible gives us. This lesson will present a sampling of those verses in an attempt to show the scope and depth of the Holy Spirit and his work.

Key Scriptures: Genesis 1:1–2, 26–27; 3:15—The difficulty of trying to fully understand God.

1. The existence and nature of God are not revealed by a single scripture but rather are revealed throughout the scriptures in many and various ways. As noted in the last lesson, Paul says that God's judgments are unsearchable and that his paths are beyond tracing out (Rom. 11:33).

2. The three "persons" of the one God, often called the "Trinity," arguably are mentioned in the first and third chapters of the Bible. This interpretation is suggested, as God further reveals himself throughout scripture this way. In Genesis 1, we see God creating the world and the "Spirit of God hovering" over creation. Additionally, in Genesis 3:15 as previously discussed, a promise is given concerning a son to be born of a woman who would be the "Seed Promise," which was finally fulfilled in Jesus. The apostles John and Paul also both refer to Jesus as the Creator (John 1:1–3 and Col. 1:16). Why do you think understanding an all-powerful, eternal God might be a bit more complicated than we would prefer it to be?

   _____
   _____

3. In Genesis 1:26; 3:22; 11:7; and Isaiah 6:8, the Bible uses plural pronouns in reference to the one God. These four verses are the only ones in scripture that do this. The meaning of this pronoun usage is debated among Christians and Jews alike. However, it does suggest that God has a more majestic, mysterious, and complicated nature than we might initially think. It can certainly be argued that God refers to himself as multiple persons in one God. Consider for a few minutes why you think God might have referred to himself as "us."

   _____
   _____

4. Read Matt 28:18–20. Jesus said he had been given all authority in heaven and on earth—total authority. Then he tells the apostles to baptize people in the name of the Father, the Son, and the Holy Spirit ("name" = "the author" = "whose *author*ity they will make disciples under"). God is revealed in the New Testament as being expressed in three persons—God the Father, God the Son, and God the Holy Spirit. Since Jesus had been given "all authority in heaven and on earth," why do you suppose he told his disciples to baptize in the name of (or by the authority of) the Father, the Son, and the Holy Spirit?

   _____
   _____
   _____

5. Read Colossians 2:9. Paul reveals that the fullness of Deity dwelled in Jesus. This is translated variously as, "God's whole nature," "the fullness of the Godhead," and "the fullness of deity." Relate this scripture to the previous ones.
   _____
   _____
   _____

6. If the fullness of God lived in Jesus Christ, then might it be reasonable to think that when something is done in the name of the Father, the Son, and the Holy Spirit, it is the same as doing it in the name of Jesus?
   _____
   _____
   _____

Further Study

1. Read 2 Corinthians 13:14. As Paul concludes this letter, notice the three persons of God he mentions. What significance do you think should be placed on what he wishes for them from each person of God (grace, love, and fellowship)?
   _____
   _____

2. Read John 14:9–11 and consider the implications of what Jesus says here. Summarize what you think Jesus is saying.
   _____
   _____

3. Read John 17:20–21. In praying for the complete unity of believers, Jesus said that his prayer was that the believers would be one just as he (Jesus) and the Father were one. Consider the implication to the nature of God from this text. How do you think Jesus, as the Son, can be one with the Father and yet still be distinct from him?
   _____
   _____

Key Scripture: John 16:13—The Holy Spirit is a "person" and not an "it."

1. The apostle John refers to the Holy Spirit as not an "it" but as a "he." The Holy Spirit is a person and not a thing.
   a. Why do you think we often hear the Holy Spirit referred to as an "it" both in church and with other Christians?
   _____
   _____
   _____

    b. Why do you think this might matter?

2. Consider the follow attributes of the Holy Spirit as a "person."
    a. He is a person—John 14:16–17; 15:26
    b. He is eternal—Hebrews 9:14
    c. He is omniscient (knows all)—1 Corinthians 2:10
    d. He is omnipotent (all-powerful)—Zechariah 4:6
    e. He is omnipresent (present everywhere)—Psalms 139:7
    f. He speaks—1 Timothy 4:1
    g. He comforts—John 14:16–17
    h. He testifies—John 15:26
    i. He guides—John 16:13
    j. He leads—Romans 8:14
    k. He possesses a mind—Romans 8:27
    l. He has knowledge—1 Corinthians 2:11
    m. He has affections—Romans 15:30
    n. He possesses a will—1 Corinthians 12:11
    o. He can be grieved—Ephesians 4:30
    p. He can be lied to—Acts 5:3
    q. He can be blasphemed—Matthew 12:32
3. What conclusions might be reached concerning the person and nature of the Holy Spirit when considering these verses collectively?

Further Study

1. Read John 14:23.
    a. What does Jesus promise that he and the Father would do for those who obey him?

    b. Given that the Holy Spirit is a fulfillment of God's promise to live within us, what does that tell us about how the "fullness of God" works in us today as believers (see also Col. 1:19 and Eph. 3:19)?

2. Read Colossians 1:26–27. What is the mystery mentioned here, and what does it mean?

Key Verse: Matt 3:16–17—The Holy Spirit's work in Jesus.

1. The Holy Spirit was seen descending on Jesus at his baptism in the form of a dove, and he continued working in Christ's life throughout his ministry.
   a. What do you think the significance is of this event?

   b. Whose sake was it for: Jesus? John the Baptist? Perhaps others around? Explain.

   c. Since Jesus was "conceived of the Holy Spirit" (Matt. 1:18), do you think it possible this was the first time Jesus was filled with him, or otherwise what is up with this?

   d. Why do you think he came on him only after Jesus had been baptized?

   e. Might Jesus's own baptism be a visual foreshadowing of what Christian baptism would be and mean? Explain.

2. Consider the following scriptures concerning Jesus and the Holy Spirit.
   a. Isaiah 11:1–2—Isaiah prophesied about the presence of the Spirit in Jesus.
   b. Matthew 4:1—The Spirit led Jesus.
   c. Luke 4:4, 18—He strengthened Jesus in his ministry.
   d. Acts 1:2—Jesus gave instructions through the Spirit.
   e. Hebrews 9:13–14—The Spirit was active at the cross.
3. What do you think these verses collectively can tell us about the Holy Spirit and his role in the life of Christ?

4. Why do you think the Spirit came in the form of a dove (see also Isa. 9:6 and Eph. 2:14)?
___
___
___

Further Study

1. Read Acts 2:37–39 (Note: this text will be dealt with to a greater degree later in this lesson). Peter promised that the Holy Spirit would be given to all believers. Given the role of the Spirit in Jesus's life, what do you think the implications are to each of our lives as disciples?
___
___
___

2. Correlate again the baptism Peter that commands of us with Christ's own baptism.
___
___
___

3. Read 1 Corinthians 2:9–16. What does Paul say the Spirit does for us, and why is this so vital to us in following Christ?
___
___
___

Key Verses: Joel 2:28–32; Acts 2:1–21; 10:23–48—The promised outpouring of the Holy Spirit.

1. Take the time to read all of these verses. As recorded in these scriptures, the outpouring of the Holy Spirit was promised in the Old Testament and the fulfillment of that promise is seen in the New Testament.
2. Read Acts 1:8 and then review Acts 2:1–21. Describe in your own words what happened to the apostles in this story?
___
___
___

3. How did Peter connect the event with what was prophesied in the book of Joel?
___
___
___

4. Read Acts 10:23–48 and Acts 11:15–18. The apostles, who were baptized with the Spirit as recorded in Acts 2, were Jews and their inclusion in the kingdom was expected. However, Cornelius and his household were not Jews and their inclusion was unexpected by the Jews. Why is it significant that the Holy Spirit "fell" on them *before* Peter and his coworkers agreed to their baptisms?

5. What was the evidence that the Spirit had "fallen" on them and why is that significant?

6. The only time that Jesus apparently baptized people with the Holy Spirit before their water baptism was in Acts 2 and Acts 10. This was done, among other things, to clearly symbolize his inclusion of both Jews and Gentiles into his body, the church. And it is the Holy Spirit that ultimately baptizes us into Christ's body (see 1 Cor. 12:12–13). Why is it important that in these two instances, the Holy Spirit came directly from Jesus who was in heaven rather than as a direct result of the apostles praying for the Spirit to come or by their laying on of hands?

Further Study

1. Read Acts 8:1–19. There is a lot being described in this text, but, specifically, when and how did the Holy Spirit "come on" the Samaritan converts and at whose prompting?

2. Read Acts 19:1–7. In his journeys, Paul found twelve men in Ephesus who had been followers of John the Baptist and had received his baptism, which was only for repentance. After Paul baptized them in the name of Jesus, he laid his hands on them. What happened right after, and why was that important to them?

3. Why is it significant that in most of the other conversion accounts that are recorded in Acts, it is not noted that hands were laid on the converts, or that they had specific "experiences" with the Spirit (review Acts 2:36–40; 8:36–39; 9:17–19; 16:13–15; 16:29–34; 18:8)?

4. The baptism with the Holy Spirit and the gift of the Holy Spirit are from Jesus *alone*. Why might each of the following points be important to our understanding of the Holy Spirit's activities today?
   a. It was Jesus who baptized the apostles and the Gentile converts of Cornelius's household with the Holy Spirit. The Spirit came directly from Jesus not through any specific act of any of the apostles.

   b. However, in the case of the converted Samaritans as well as the converts at Ephesus, the Spirit came on them at the laying on of the apostles' hands.

   c. In 1 Corinthians 12:11, we see the Spirit giving certain gifts to the Christians in Corinth.

   d. Thus it might be concluded that it is Jesus who gives the Spirit to us, and it is the Spirit that gives us supernatural experiences and ministry gifts.

Key Verse: Acts 2:38–39—The promise of the Holy Spirit is to all.

1. The promise of the Holy Spirit is given to all who are called by God and who accept Jesus Christ as Lord and Savior.
2. In 1 Corinthians 6:19–20, the apostle Paul says that each believer's body is literally a temple of the Holy Spirit of God. Since the fall of man in the Garden of Eden, humankind had been separated from God in a variety of ways and to varying degrees. Even though the Israelites were God's chosen people, they often interacted with him in very impersonal ways (e.g., Exod. 20:18). Why would the promise of the Spirit living personally within each believer be so significant to the original hearers?

3. Read Romans 8:9 and 2 Corinthians 13:5. What does Paul say about believers who do not have the Holy Spirit in them?

4. If the Spirit lives in us what does that imply about Jesus living in us?

5. Read again the key verses in Acts 2:36–39. The Spirit is received by the work of Christ through our rebirth, which involves faith, repentance, and baptism. Although each of these subjects was explored more deeply in Lesson 8, consider carefully the original promise Peter gave to all believers. Write in your own words the meaning of each verse.

Further Study

1. In Acts 2:16–20, Peter quotes a prophecy from Joel 2:28–32. The promise was that God was going to pour out his Spirit on "all people." Compare the promise in Acts 2:39 with this promise in Joel 2.

2. Read Acts 10:34. Note the conclusion that Peter was brought to concerning God's promise to people everywhere. In Acts 2:16–20, Peter quotes a prophecy from Joel 2:28–32. The promise was that God was going to pour out his Spirit on "all people." Compare the promise in Acts 2:39 with this promise in Joel 2.

Key Verses: Luke 11:9–13 and Acts 5:27–32—Christ gives the Holy Spirit to those who ask for him and to those who obey God.

1. Notice the Bible text surrounding Luke 11:13.
    a. The context is Jesus's promise that whoever seeks God will find God. How then can we tell if we or others are genuinely seeking God? (see James 4:1–3 for some explanation and help)?

    b. What point is Jesus making about how the Father treats his children and how does it relate to our reception of the Holy Spirit?

c. How would you describe the kind of request for the Holy Spirit that the Father would likely respond best to?

_____
_____
_____

2. Read Acts 5:27–32.
   a. Obedience to God is a broad concept. What was going on in this instance that led Peter to say that God gives the Holy Spirit to those that obey him?

   _____
   _____
   _____

   b. The issue involved was that the Sanhedrin (the Jewish ruling council) had ordered the apostles not to preach Christ any longer, and yet they were continuing to do just that.
      i. The question the apostles posed was whether they should obey men (the Sanhedrin) or they should obey God, who had commanded them to preach Christ.
      ii. It was in the Great Commission, which Jesus had given to the apostles (Matt. 28:19–20), that he had promised them that if they would go preach to all nations, he would perpetually be with Christians throughout this age. What does it mean for Christ to "be with" someone in the way he promises here?

      _____
      _____
      _____

      iii. What kind of obedience do you think Peter was speaking about that would bring the Holy Spirit from God?

      _____
      _____
      _____

Further Study

1. In scripture there are two kinds of "works."
   a. One kind is of the legalistic variety where the worker is trying to achieve or earn rightness with God through performance. Legalists are often seeking the praise or approval of other people, whether wittingly or unwittingly.
      i. Jesus perhaps mentions this kind of person in Matthew 7:22–23.
      ii. These kinds of works are what constitute an attempt at "salvation by works" (Eph. 2:8–9).
2. The negative kind of "obedience" is what legalism is all about. It is about doing the right things but for the wrong motives.
3. Works are not able to earn us salvation, nor is obedience able to merit it for us. In fact, works that are done in order to merit something from God are counter to the essence of faith itself. Why is this so?

_____
_____
_____

4. The other kind of work and obedience are simply the response of faith.
   a. James carefully explains that this is the kind of work that in fact validates our faith (James 2:14–26). He says, "As the body without the spirit is dead, so faith without deeds is dead" (verse 26). What does this mean?
   _____
   _____
   _____

   b. John says the right kind of obedience is, in fact, what confirms that we have true faith. Read 1 John 2:3–6. He makes it clear that persons who claim to know Christ but do not obey him are lying to themselves and to others. He also says that it is in our obedience to God that love is made complete in us. How is this counter to what many Christians believe today?
   _____
   _____
   _____

   c. In scripture faith and obedience are inseparable. True faith (which involves trust) will always lead one to give a best effort at obedience to God. The acts of obedience themselves have nothing to do with earning salvation, but they have everything to do with their witness to the actuality of the faith that is being claimed. On the other hand, a lack of faith and disobedience are equated in Hebrews 3:18–19. Why might it be said that a lack of faith and disobedience are relatively equal?
   _____
   _____
   _____

5. What kind of "asking" do you believe God will most respond to in terms of giving us the Holy Spirit?
   _____
   _____
   _____

6. What kind of "obeying" do you believe God will most respond to in terms of giving us the Holy Spirit?
   _____
   _____
   _____

Key Verse: Romans 8—The Holy Spirit actively works in Christians' lives to fulfill God's purposes for them.

1. Review Romans 8 and note all the verses associated with the work of the Holy Spirit in our lives.
   a. He is called the Spirit of life that sets us free, verse 2 (see also 2 Cor. 3:17).
   b. The requirements of the Law are fully met for us when we live by the Spirit, verse 4.
   c. He validates that we belong to God, verses 9–10.
   d. He is the only way we can overcome our sinful nature, verse 13.
   e. The Spirit's leadership in our lives is the proof of our sonship in Christ, verses 14–16.
   f. He helps us in our weaknesses, verse 26.
   g. He intercedes for us in prayer, verses 26–27.

2. There are numerous passages that tell of the Spirit's work in believers. Briefly write the implications of each of these to your own life.
   a. Regenerates us—John 3:5

   b. Convicts and guides us—John 16:8, 13

   c. Brings freedom to us—2 Corinthians 3:17

   d. Transforms us and conforms us to Christ—2 Corinthians 3:18

   e. Sanctifies us—Romans 15:16

   f. Empowers us to understand God—1 Corinthians 2:13

   g. Intercedes for us with God—Romans 8:26

   h. Unifies us—1 Corinthians 12:12 and Ephesians 4:3

   i. The Father and the Son live and work in us through the Holy Spirit—John 14:23 and Philippians 2:14

   j. The Spirit also empowers us to:
      i. Experience God's incredible love and grace—Ephesians 3:16–21

ii. Perform works of ministry—some that might be seen as "miraculous" and others that are seen as "giftedness"—1 Corinthians 12:11

iii. Overcome sin and the sinful world—Romans 8:13

iv. Flow from us to others—John 7:38

v. Bear spiritual fruit—Galatians 5:22–23

vi. Exercise our ministry gifts—1 Corinthians 12:4–7

3. Note also the warnings God gives to each of us concerning the Spirit and consider the meaning of each.
   a. He can be grieved—Ephesians 4:30

   b. He can be resisted—Acts 5:3

   c. His fire in us can be put out—1 Thessalonians 5:19

Key Verse: 1 Corinthians 13:7–13—Faith, hope, and love are the Spirit's greatest gifts, and love is the greatest of these three.

1. It is easy to become enamored with the powerful things that the Holy Spirit can gift us to do. However, the ultimate, most miraculous, and most enduring gifts of the Spirit on earth are faith, hope, and love.

Comparing faith, hope, and love with prophesying, speaking in tongues, healing, and so forth, why do you suppose faith, hope, and love in and among us are the more miraculous of all these gifts?

2. Jesus indicates that over the course of time certain of these revelatory gifts (tongues, prophecy, gifts of special spiritual knowledge) would cease. What three gifts does he say will remain?

3. Why do you think these are the three gifts that will remain supreme even before the return of Christ? (hint: consider the definitions of faith and hope and how they too will disappear when Christ returns, Heb. 11:1)

4. Read Gal 5:22–24. List all the attributes of the Holy Spirit's fruit that *he* will bear in our lives as we follow Christ.

Further Study

1. Read 1 John 4:8.
   a. What does John say is the very essence of God?

   b. Why then is growing in love the greatest of the miracles?

   c. Might one perform certain miracles or powerful works and not even have a relationship with God (review Matt. 7:21–23)?

2. Read Ephesians 5:1–2. If we are filled with the Spirit, we will be empowered to imitate Christ. When we imitate Christ what kind of lives will we live?

3. Read Romans 8:1–5. Where does the apostle Paul say our hope and love both come from?

Self-Reflection

1. How does the Spirit come to live in us and who is it that gives him to you?

2. In your own words, how can you expect the Spirit to grow and change you?

3. How does this study affect or change your views on the Holy Spirit?

4. What actions might you need to take in regard to this lesson?

5. What questions do you still have concerning the person and work of the Holy Spirit?

LESSON 10
Reflections on Encountering Christ: Stories of Encounters with Jesus

Introduction

Man looks at outward appearances, but God sees directly into our hearts. Although who we are outwardly will ultimately reveal who we are inwardly, in brief encounters looks can be very deceiving concerning what is inside. We can fool others. We can fool ourselves. But we cannot fool God. God is looking for hearts that are seeking him. God is looking for hearts of devotion. In the beginning and in the end, God views the veracity of our faith from the inside out. He knows the reality as only he can.

The gospel writers give us many examples of people encountering Christ. Some are direct encounters and some are indirect ones. Not only do we come to see the external, life circumstances of these individuals, but also we often are allowed to briefly get glimpses into the hearts and lives of these individuals as they encounter Jesus. The stories chosen below are intended for use as examples that will give us insight into our own hearts. The purpose of this lesson is to help us readjust our own thinking and allow God to change our hearts as we discover and encounter him, whether we are already a Christian or whether we are seeking or approaching him for the first time. In each text, consider what went right or what went wrong. Consider what kind of heart and attitude pleases him and what kind repels him. Consider how those who pleased him approached him. And consider how these right attitudes and behaviors might look in your own life today. The beginning of your own encounter with Jesus has likely already occurred or is just now occurring. Consider how the story of your own encounter with Christ might read up to this point in time? Ponder for a moment how you want the story of your encounter with him to end, because God is at present giving you some say in it.

Before launching into the study, take a moment to read the following poem written to describe a desperate woman's encounter with Jesus.

Touching God
(Mark 5:24–31; Matt. 9:20–26; Luke 8:40–56)

I was alone and rejected, and really even worse than that,
I was unclean, untouchable, and desperate.
For years I'd begged God for healing and seen many doctors,
But for my suffering there was simply no respite!

My husband had left me, and by the Law was justified,
My children would see me, but from only across the room,
I had grandchildren I had never even touched,
My life was only loneliness, despair, and gloom.

Plus, I was so weak, wan, and washed out,
Pale, emaciated, hurting, and usually quite ill,
For me there was never a hopeful answer,
My battle had long been only steep and uphill.

Even the doctors had given up on me,
Told me never to come to them again,
The treatments were intolerable anyway,
They said my suffering was due to my own sin.

I was not even permitted in the synagogue,
Where all my friends most likely were just now!
However, I'd heard Jesus was headed that way,
And, I must hurry and get to him somehow!

I pulled myself up and carefully prepared to go,
First of all to cover my ugly bleeding,
Then I would discreetly hide who I even was,
Obscure to all what I was actually needing.

For me to even touch another,
Would make them be "unclean,"
So I could only in stealth touch him,
To avoid an embarrassing scene!

With scarcely none of my face showing,
I pressed in through the frenzied crowd,
I saw the face of Jesus in the middle,
Of this jumbled mass so bold and loud.

His face showed through like a beacon,
As he headed resolutely right by me,
I'd seen and heard him from afar before,
At least two times and maybe now three.

The crowd pushed in as he walked our way,
In determination I held my ground and pressed still nearer.

He definitely looked a prophet and more,
That he must be Messiah was now ever clearer!

I looked down to hide as he walked by me;
Then I reached out and touched but his fringe.
But the jolt I felt to my heart's very core,
Almost caused me to completely unhinge!

As I felt and just "knew" what had happened;
Spontaneously started inwardly celebrating,
He started looking all around and then right at me;
This powerful man was clearly deliberating!

I couldn't hear him, but I read his lips:
"Who touched my clothes?" he was saying.
I was backing away so deftly now,
To answer him, I was obviously delaying.

He said, "Someone touched me; I felt power go out."
They all denied it in confusion and clamor.
I knew then I could not go unnoticed any longer,
I looked at him and spoke with stammer.

The look in his eyes was magnetic though;
His amazing glow was so completely enthralling.
The look of love in his eyes, I'll never forget,
As at his feet I was trembling and falling!

I was begging in fear of what was to come,
At the scene that I was now causing:
Jesus was headed to heal a ruler's dying child,
Now I had openly caused his pausing!

To him I muttered quickly the whole truth,
In shock I told him my whole tale.
I told him I'd cried out for God's help,
As I whispered beneath my humiliation's wail.

In an instant I had been completely healed!
I told him what had just been done.
He spoke not as a mortal man,
He was the Messiah; this was surely God's Son!

Just then the ruler was told his daughter had died,
While Jesus's visit she was direly awaiting!
The man looked at me in bitter anger and hurt,
For my causing his deliverer's hesitating.

But Jesus ignored his obvious ire,
Then looked directly down at me.
I had clearly made myself such a fool,
For my whole cold world to see!

But not a voice dared to rise,
As the crowd's power his words stole,
"Daughter, go in peace and be free,
Your faith has made you whole!"

While he was still speaking, some men ran up,
And told the man Jarius his daughter had died,
But Jesus said boldly and confidently to them there,
"Just believe," then as he walked away, he just sighed.

I quickly raced away then and ran right home,
Locked the door and sat down in shock.
The bleeding had stopped; the pain completely gone!
Then I heard at the door their knock!

A small gang stood together at my door,
Some with questions; some still seething.
I explained to them how by Jesus I had been completely healed,
Midst my fearful, panicked breathing!

I was welcomed back into the synagogue,
I heard the child, when Jesus had gotten there, had arisen!
We both had been freed from our bondage here,
Released from pain's darkened prison!

I lived out my life; got my family back,
The day I risked all to touch Messiah,
Such a simple touch, in desperation for sure,
Ended my life as a broken pariah!

So the day I was healed, I remember so well,
I was surely not proper and prim,
But it was not the day that God touched me,
It was the day that I touched him!

Encounters with Christ:

1. Alone and hurting—bleeding woman: Mark 5:24–31; Matt. 9:20–26; Luke 8:40–56
   a. Describe the woman and her problem.

   b. In what ways can you relate to her? Have you ever "bled" in some secret and perhaps embarrassing way and either withdrew from others out of fear or felt an outcast by others? How does that sort of helplessness and hopelessness affect your life and personality?

   c. How did she approach Jesus and why?

   d. What was Christ's response to her?

   e. What are the key lessons for us?

2. Two men called by Jesus—Philip and Nathanael: John 1:43–51
   a. Describe the situation.

   b. Describe Philip and Nathaniel? (It is believed by many that Nathaniel is the apostle also known as Bartholomew.)

   c. How did Philip initially encounter Christ?

   d. What did Philip then go and do?

e. How did Nathaniel encounter Christ?

f. Describe the exchange between Jesus and Nathaniel and what its significance is.

g. What did Jesus commend Nathaniel for and what does it mean?

h. What are the key lessons?

3. Mary as a mother—Jesus's mother at wedding feast: John 2:1–11
   a. Describe the situation.

   b. How did Mary get involved?

   c. How did she involve her son Jesus?

   d. What was her approach with him?

   e. What was Christ's initial response to her?

   f. How did she respond to that?

g. What did Jesus end up doing?

h. Why do you think he did that?

i. What might this encounter with his own mother suggest about Jesus?

j. What might this story tell about the supernatural components in the relationship between Mary and her son Jesus? For instance, how did she know he could "fix" the wine problem, and why would she be so inclined to seemingly "force" him into it?

k. What are the other lessons that might be gleaned from this?

4. A sick desperate one—the leprous man: Matthew 8:1–4; Luke 5:12–14
   a. Describe the man, his situation, and his encounter with Jesus.

   b. How did the leper approach Christ?

   c. What was Christ's response to him?

   d. At what points have you felt desperation; thus, in what ways can you relate to some as desperate as a leprous person likely would be during Jesus's time?

e. What might be some spiritual and physical parallels to this story today that could lead any one of us to the kind of hopelessness this man must surely have felt? How might encountering Christ bring healing to such as these today, just as it brought healing to the leper?

f. What then are the key lessons for us from this encounter—lessons for down and hurting people, lessons for those not currently in trial, and lessons about Jesus?

5. A powerful but helpless outsider—the Roman Centurion: Matthew 8:5–13: Luke 7:1–10
    a. Describe the Centurion and his likely relationship with the Jews. Use any of the Bible sources online to get a good description.

    b. What was the problem he was asking help with?

    c. How does Matthew's telling of the story differ from Luke's?

    d. When Jesus went to the Centurion's, what was it the man said to him?

    e. How did Christ respond to him?

    f. What do you think was going on in the man's heart that drove Jesus to respond in such a way to his request?

    g. What are some key lessons?

6. A woman out of place—the Canaanite woman: Matthew 15:21–28; Mark 7:24–30
   a. Describe the woman.

   b. How did she approach Jesus at first?

   c. What was his initial response, and why did he respond in that way?

   d. What was her next approach?

   e. What was Christ's response to that?

   f. How did this woman find favor with Christ?

   g. What are the key lessons?

7. A good kid—the rich young man: Matthew 19:16–24
   a. Describe the young man.

   b. Describe the situation.

   c. How did the young man approach Jesus?

d. What do you think he was wanting from Jesus?

e. How can you personally relate to this guy?

f. What was Christ's response to him initially and then finally?

g. What are the key lessons?

8. A proud mom—the mother of James and John: Matthew 20:20–28
   a. Describe the mother and what she was asking of Jesus.

   b. What was Christ's response to her?

   c. What concerns do most parents have for their children that may cause their prayers and requests to resonate with the same motives of this mother?

   d. What is the ignorance and desperation in such desires and prayers?

   e. What are the key lessons for us?

9. A "little" guy—Zacchaeus: Luke 19:1–10
   a. Describe the situation.

b. Who was Zacchaeus, and why is this relevant to the story? (If you don't already know about it, look up some information about who the tax collectors (publicans) were during Jesus's day and how the Jews generally felt about them and why.)

c. Might Zacchaeus's small stature be somewhat metaphorical for this man's inner self-esteem? How might this be so?

d. What did Zacchaeus do that drew Jesus's attention?

e. What was Christ's initial response to him?

f. How does Luke describe Zacchaeus's response to Jesus's call to him?

g. What did Jesus say in response to that?

h. What key lessons do you glean from this encounter?

10. A bold beggar—a blind man: Mark 10:46–52
    a. Describe the situation.

    b. Ponder for a few moments what life must have been like for a blind person during Jesus's time. Visualize his helplessness, his dependence on others, and his social status. Now describe what must have been going on with this particular blind person, a man identified as named Bartimaeus.

c. How did the man "approach" Jesus?

d. How did many of the people around react to the man?

e. What was Christ's response to him?

f. What are the key lessons?

11. A widow's offering: Mark 12:41–44
    a. Describe the situation.

    b. This was an encounter with Jesus that this poor widow was likely unaware of. However, Jesus was aware, was he not? How might each of us have encounters with Jesus of which we are unaware?

    c. What does it say about all the rich members of a closely knit synagogue that this widow had so little money in the first place?

    d. Describe the widow's offering?

    e. What was Christ's response to her offering?

f. How do you suppose this widow's unaware encounter with Christ has impacted so many people over the centuries?

g. What are the key lessons?

12. A man of importance—Nicodemus of the Sanhedrin: John 3:1–15
    a. Describe the situation.

    b. Who was Nicodemus and why was it significant that he approached Jesus at all?

    c. What is the significance of his visit being at night?

    d. What was Nicodemus's initial approach?

    e. How did Jesus initially respond?

    f. How did Nicodemus react to that?

    g. What was Jesus's response to that?

    h. What are the key lessons derived from Nicodemus about ourselves and about Jesus?

13. Two dear friends of Jesus—Mary and Martha: Luke 10:38–42
    a. Describe the situation.

    b. Describe how the two women are depicted?

    c. How did Martha approach Jesus?

    d. What was Mary doing, and how did Jesus feel about that?

    e. What was Christ's response to Martha and Mary?

    f. Can you think of some present-day situations that might be similar to this—at home, in the workplace, in religious contexts, and so forth?

    g. What is the key lesson?

14. A double outcast—the Samaritan woman: John 4:7–26
    a. Describe the situation.

    b. Why did the woman end up encountering Jesus in the first place?

    c. Why was Jesus's conversation with her a big deal?

d. How did Christ approach her?

e. How did she respond to him?

f. What was his response to her?

g. What did she ultimately do in response to her encounter with Jesus?

h. What are the key lessons?

15. A helpless person—a man paralyzed for thirty-eight years : John 5:1–15
    a. Describe the situation.

    b. Describe the paralytic.

    c. How did the man encounter Jesus?

    d. How did Jesus respond to him?

    e. What was the man's excuse?

f. What did Jesus tell him to do?

g. What did the man do?

h. How can you relate to this man in his encounter with Jesus?

i. What are the key lessons?

16. Unbelieving disciples: John 6:25–69
    a. Describe the situation and what the disciples were reacting to.

    b. What were the disciples saying and reacting so negatively to and why?

    c. What did many of the disciples end up doing?

    d. What was Christ's response to the twelve apostles?

    e. How did Peter respond to Jesus (apparently speaking on behalf of the rest of them)?

    f. If you are a Christian already, how might you have felt and reacted similarly about what Jesus asks of you?

g. What are the key lessons?

17. A woman humiliated and some condemning, unbelieving men—an adulterous woman made an example by some men who would be humbled: John 8: 1–11
    a. Describe the situation.

    b. Describe the woman and how she came to encounter Christ.

    c. Describe her accusers.

    d. By the way, where do you suppose the man was with whom she had been committing adultery?

    e. How did her accusers approach Jesus?

    f. What was the real reason they were bringing the woman to Jesus?

    g. What was Christ's response to their challenge?

    h. How did the accusers react to that?

    i. What happened then?

j. What was the exchange Jesus and the woman then had?

k. How can you relate to this woman, personally or because of some situation you know about?

l. What are the key lessons?

18. A daring person—the woman with the expensive perfume: Mark 14:3–9; Luke 7:36–50
    a. Describe the situation.

    b. How did the woman approach Jesus?

    c. Why does her approach and timing seem particularly bold?

    d. How did those around respond to her generous offering?

    e. What do you think their real problem might have been?

    f. How did Jesus respond to the other people?

    g. What was Christ's response to her?

h. In Mark 14:11-12, read what follows this story. What important event in Jesus's life might have been prompted by this particular encounter, and what might be any significance of this?

i. What are the key lessons?

19. A friend who failed—Peter's denial: Mark 14:66–72; Matthew 26:69–75
    a. Describe the situation.

    b. Who was Peter and what was his relationship to Jesus?

    c. What did Peter do that caused Christ to look at him the way he likely did?

    d. What was Christ's response to what Peter did?

    e. How did it impact Peter?

    f. The gospels and Acts clearly explain that Jesus came back to Peter, Peter repented, and Jesus completely restored him to his relationship and ministry. What does this tell us about Peter, and what does this tell us about Jesus?

    g. What are other key lessons?

20. A man with evil intent—Judas Iscariot: Matthew 26:14–16, 47–57; 27:1–5
    a. Describe the situation.

    b. Describe Judas and his relationship with Jesus.

    c. Why did Judas do what he did?

    d. What was Christ's response to Judas when Judas led the authorities to arrest Jesus?

    e. How did Judas ultimately feel about his betrayal of Jesus, and what did he finally do (read Matt. 27:1–10)?

    f. What are the key lessons from the story of Judas?

21. A man worthy of his death—a thief on the cross next to Jesus: Luke 23:32–43
    a. Describe the situation.

    b. Describe the men on each side of Jesus?

    c. How and why did the man address Jesus?

    d. What do you think he might have already known or not known about Jesus, what was he asking for, and what do you think he expected?

e. How "spiritual" do you think his request really was?

f. What was Christ's response to him?

g. What lessons do you think are intended to emerge from this story?

22. One struggling with the unbelievable—doubting Thomas: John 20:24–29
    a. Describe the situation.

    b. What do you think Thomas was like?

    c. Why was Thomas doubtful?

    d. How does Thomas's attitude exist somewhere in all of us, and why?

    e. What was Christ's response to Thomas on Jesus's second appearance to the apostles when Thomas was present?

    f. How did Thomas respond to Jesus at that point?

    g. What blessing did Jesus pronounce on all of us who have not gotten to see him visually?

h. What are other key lessons?

23. Saul who became the apostle Paul: Acts 9:1–19 (see also Paul's recounting of his early encounter with Jesus in Acts 22:1–21 and Acts 26:1–23)
    a. Describe the situation.

    b. Describe Saul.

    c. Describe how Jesus encountered Saul.

    d. Describe Saul's response to Jesus.

    e. What happened next?

    f. Describe Saul's acceptance of Christ.

    g. How did Jesus continue working with Saul?

    h. Read 2 Timothy 4:17 and the statement Paul makes concerning his relationship with Jesus at that point. What does that tell us about how Saul's encounter ended up?

    i. What are the key lessons?

Self-Reflection

1. How might I have previously encountered Jesus in my own life?

2. How did I act and react?

3. What about my heart may have been right?

4. What about my heart may have not been so right?

5. Where am I now in my encounters with Christ?

6. Which of the encounters in this lesson do I most relate to and why?

7. What actions might I take that will lead me to more positive encounters with Jesus?

8. What is my own responsibility in getting my heart right in my relationship with Christ?

9. What can I expect from God in regard to getting my heart right?

LESSON 11
The Body of Christ, the Church: Living in the Community of Christ

INTRODUCTION

ONE OF THE GREAT REVELATIONS of the New Testament is that when we become a part of Christ we become a part of his actual body, which is his church. The Holy Spirit, whom Christ sends us at our conversion, adds us to the body of Christ (1 Cor. 12:13). Our participation in the body of Christ is shown to be much more than mere "church membership" or attendance, as many seem to think. To Christ, it is much, much more than that—it is a spiritual and supernatural fellowship, or literally a partnership, in which all Christians share in the "here-and-now present-day manifestation" of Christ in the world. Individual Christians will manifest Christ in many ways, while living out his mission, because of the Holy Spirit living in us. However, the full manifestation of Christ is only to be achieved by the collective partnership/fellowship of his church, locally and universally. The church, the body of Christ, does this in this world by the love it expresses, the good it does, and the light it manifests (John 13:34–35; Eph. 2:10; Matt. 5:14–16). However, perhaps even more importantly, the church shows Christ's glory by being a demonstration of how amazing his grace is for his people, the church (Eph. 2:6–7). The church was not built to show its own goodness, but rather to show the goodness of Christ, so that the world may be drawn to him and come to trust only in *his* love and goodness, rather than seeking the self-reliance and self-determination of the deadly forbidden fruit.

The body of Christ also functions collectively for the spiritual and physical health and well-being of its member parts. As with our physical bodies, the parts of the spiritual body need each other to live and function properly (1 Cor. 12:12–13). Yet sadly, many have come to the deceitful conclusion that church membership and participation is optional and unnecessary—that Christianity is simply about me, me, me, and my own all-important relationship with God. This selfish, self-centered brand of pseudo-Christianity is in fact the very antithesis of the nature and purpose of Christ! Perhaps a casual participation is "optional," if one is merely attending and not really participating in the body anyway. However, in God's design, when we commit to follow Christ we are committing to be a part of his body—the church of Jesus Christ! If we are truly following Christ, we will be instantly led to Christ's church. Nearly every core command of Christ will necessitate our gravitation toward his church. If any of us is not feeling led to the body of Christ, we should suspect that Christ is not leading us at all! One simply will not be able to honestly lay claim to faithful obedience outside of the context of the spiritual, Christian community. Any broad rejection of the church due to its imperfections and failings will demonstrate our own failure to offer the grace to others that Christ has offered to us all!

The purpose of this lesson is to show the essential and vital nature of the body of Christ in the daily lives of Christ's disciples. Also it will explore the purposes and functions of the church for the members as well as for the world itself. As you have likely already observed, at this point and beyond in these lessons, repetition is inevitable and necessary in establishing new or additional ideas and points. If certain portions of the information are already clear to you, though, simply review it and move on.

Key Scripture: Matthew 16:13–19—Jesus is the designer and builder of his church.

1. Jesus declares that he will build his church—the temple of the Holy Spirit today on earth. Why is it important to understand that Jesus is the builder of his church, wherever it exists?

2. In this passage, Jesus is preparing the apostles for their final journey to Jerusalem, where Jesus was to face his crucifixion.
   a. The first part of the discussion is about who the people in general were saying Jesus was. Why is who we say Jesus is all-important to the faith?

   b. Then Jesus turns and asks them who they, the apostles, say Jesus is. At this Peter responds with, "You are the Christ, the Son of the living God." Why was it so profound that Peter so boldly acknowledged Jesus as the Christ, or Messiah?

   c. What do you think it meant to Peter that Jesus had the words of eternal life?

   d. Jesus then tells them he will build his church on them. How strong would one need to be to be a part of the solid foundation of the universal, perpetually growing church that Jesus would build over thousands of years? Think of all the weight their lives and testimony hold up still today in what millions of Christians believe and how we live? Think of the millions who have suffered greatly, been tortured and even killed because of the beliefs that these original apostles handed to us.

   e. Paul later explained this reality that the church, as the "household of God," was built on this foundation of these apostles and the original prophets that worked with them, with Jesus as the chief cornerstone (Eph. 2:19–22).
   f. Paul further explains that the church is a "temple of the Holy Spirit" and that God is building each believer into it. What are the implications that, as a brick in a wall, we are built into the church?

g. What does it say then when a Christian holds up no weight in the holy temple of God and is not, to any significant degree, connected to any of the other parts or the whole?
___
___

h. How would you like to live in a house where many of the parts were not connected and were often found to just be missing? Briefly explain.
___
___

i. How strong would this kind of structure be?
___
___

j. How do you think the Holy Spirit feels and functions in the church when many of the parts remain unconnected because of casual attenders and uncommitted members?
___
___

k. What is our part in getting in the place for God to build us into his temple, the church?
___
___

l. Why do you think that the confession of Jesus as the Christ and the Son of God is vital to the building of the church of Jesus Christ?
___
___

3. The Greek word that is translated "church" is the Greek word *ekklesia*. The word is made up of the Greek words *kaleo*, meaning "to call," and *ek*, meaning "out." Together they mean "the called out" or "those called out." In the English translations of the New Testament, *ekklesia* is generally translated "church," a word that in the English language originally meant the "Lord's house." Thus today, unfortunately, the word "church" is still often seen as the name for a church building, often simply called "the Lord's house." However, the church is the assembly of the called out of Christ that meet there—the body of Christ. Why do you think this distinction matters?
___
___

4. How can making this distinction about the church help us emphasize the importance of church participation with those seeking Christ or truth or with new Christians?
___
___

5. In Ephesians 1:22–23, Paul explains that Christ is the head over the church, which he says is itself the body of Christ. As mentioned, the body of Christ is spoken of as the church, the temple of the Holy Spirit, and the household of God. It is also spoken of as the Heavenly Jerusalem (Heb. 12:22), a spiritual house (1 Pet. 2:5), and the Bride of Christ (Eph. 5:25–32). Why is it important to know the various descriptive names that are used for the body?

6. What does each of these words mean, and why do we need to understand them to grow in our connectedness and functioning within the church?
    a. Church?

    b. Body of Christ?

    c. Household of God?

    d. Temple of the Holy Spirit?

    e. Spiritual house?

    f. Bride of Christ?

    g. Heavenly Jerusalem?

7. In Ephesians 2:19–22, as seen above, Paul says each member is being "built into" Christ's church. In 1 Corinthians 12:18, Paul says that God places the parts (members) into the body of Christ according to his own will. As Christ said he would, he is building his church. How should this affect each disciple's view of planting, growing, developing, and unifying churches?

___

8. The phrase "body of Christ," seen metaphorically, helps us to see that the church is the physical representation of Christ on earth.
    a. It also demonstrates that there are different roles members play as parts of the body and thus our essential interdependence on one another (1 Cor. 12:14–17, 27). Explain what this interdependence of functioning parts should look like?

    ___

    b. How is this idea quite different from the view so many hold of what it means to be a church member or "go to church"?

    ___

Further Study

1. Jesus built the church as the temple of the Holy Spirit.
    a. Take the time to read John 16:7; Luke 24:48–49; Acts 1:4–5; Acts 2:1–4; Acts 2:38–39; 1 Corinthians 6:19–20; and Ephesians 2:19–22.
    b. In this progression of scriptures, it can be seen that Jesus said he had to leave so that the Holy Spirit could come.
    c. After his resurrection, he told the apostles to wait in Jerusalem until they were given the Holy Spirit.
    d. Luke tells the story of the pouring out of the Holy Spirit and quotes Peter, saying that the Holy Spirit was promised to all whom God calls.
    e. Paul says that individually as Christians our bodies are temples of the Holy Spirit.
    f. How do you think Jesus continues working through the Holy Spirit to build up his church individually and collectively?

    ___

2. Considering the finiteness and the earthly limitations of Jesus, in the form of a man while he was on earth, it is clear why Jesus ascended back to heaven and sent the transcendent Holy Spirit to fill the entirety of the church.

3. Read Mark 3:13–15; Ephesians 2:20. Mark records here Jesus's appointment of the twelve apostles.
    a. Mark says Jesus appointed the apostles to be with him so he could send them out. Jesus said it was he who would build his church, and this small fellowship of twelve men he put together was to be the foundation of the church—his holy temple.
    b. Since the church is supposed to follow in the footsteps of Jesus and the apostles, what characteristics do you think should be most evident in the church, and how does that compare to the average modern church?

4. To what degree and how specifically should modern churches look similar or different from Jesus's original fellowship and the initial church that the apostles built through the Holy Spirit? Explain.

Key Scripture: Acts 2:41–47—The Establishment of the Church.

1. In this passage, Luke gives the account of Jesus's formal establishment of his church. He started the work himself and he continued it through the Holy Spirit. This account gives a brief synopsis of the conversion of the first Christians—their conversions, their new lifestyles, and the dynamics and attributes of the first church community.
2. Describe their conversion.

3. List all the things Luke tells us here about the characteristics of the early church.

4. How does the description of the church here compare to your own experiences or observations of most modern churches in general? For good and for bad, why do you think the church today might necessarily differ significantly from the early church?

5. In verse 42, Luke tells that, "They devoted themselves…" What does the word "devoted" mean, and what evidence does Luke give demonstrating their devotion?

6. One of the things they devoted themselves to was "the fellowship."
    a. As previously explained, the Greek word for fellowship here is the word *koinónia*.
    b. Unlike the modern English word for fellowship, which often means little more than socializing, the *koinónia* literally means "a partnership."
    c. It signifies participation in, contribution to, and communion with the others.
    d. As Luke describes it, how do you see the early church function in a partnership?

    e. How can each Christian help the church to be more effective as a true fellowship?

7. How does understanding this view of the fellowship of the members with each other help us further understand the intended interdependence of the members of the body of Christ upon each other?

8. What were the other three practices they devoted themselves to (verse 42), what does each mean, and how do you see their devotion to these played out (verses 43–47)?

9. Why is it important for each of us to seek a church that strives to be this kind of fellowship and for each of us to truly devote ourselves to the fellowship?

10. However, is it possible the Spirit might lead any one of us to a church that is not functioning well, in order for us to be an influence in bringing positive change and spiritual development?

Further Study

1. Read Acts 4:32–37 and explain further the dynamic of the early church as Luke describes it.

2. What do you think prompted such generosity among the church members toward each other and the body as a whole?

3. Why do you suppose such generosity and such an attitude toward the body might be considered rare today?

4. In your estimation, what is the remedy to such a lack of generosity?

Key Verse: 1 Corinthians 12:12–27—The church functioning as a body.

1. In response to tremendous division in the Corinthians church (1 Cor. 1:10), Paul explains in this text the body of Christ and how each member is a part of it.
2. Again, what is the body of Christ and what/who are its parts?

3. According to verse 18, who places the parts within the body, and what does that say about someone who seems to have no place or function in the body?

4. In your own words, what is the apostle Paul saying about the church, the body of Christ?

5. What would you say then to a Christian who wants to be a part of Christ but does not want to be a functioning member of the body?

6. What is a Christian ultimately saying to the church and the world when he/she is not part of a church body or is haphazard or negligent in participation?
   _____
   _____

7. What steps can each of us take to be a part of strengthening the devotion of individual members to effective participation (fellowship) in the body of Christ?
   _____
   _____
   _____

Further Study

1. For further emphasis on this point, consider the following passages and what each has to say about God's direct role in building the body of Christ and the implication to our own participation with him in it.
   a. Matthew 16:18
   _____
   _____

   b. Acts 2:47
   _____
   _____

   c. 1 Corinthians 12:13, 18
   _____
   _____

   d. 1 Corinthians 3:5–9
   _____
   _____

   e. Ephesians 4:3–5
   _____
   _____

2. If one is surrendered to God, what will God then do with her/him in regard to the church body?
   _____
   _____
   _____

3. Read Hebrews 10:19–25. The Hebrew letter was written to a second and third generation of Christians whose devotion to Christ and the body had clearly waned. In this text, what is the writer urging the Christians to do and to think?

   _____
   _____

4. What does it say in verse 25 concerning meeting together with the body (going to the various meetings and assemblies of the church)?

   _____
   _____

5. Note how this text connects the failure to meet with the church with deliberate sin and even the ultimate rejection of the grace of Christ (verses 26–31). Why do you believe such a strong connection might exist in this regard?

   _____
   _____
   _____

6. Read Romans 12:3–8. In describing some various gifts given to Christians, Paul states that "all the members belong to one another." In Ephesians 5:21, Paul says we are "to submit to one another out of reverence for Christ." In Romans 12:10, he says Christians should "be devoted to one another and should honor each other above self." Do you think most Christians/church members take these principles seriously? Why or why not?

   _____
   _____

7. In your own words, describe what a church body will look like when these scriptures are truly obeyed.

   _____
   _____
   _____

Key Scripture: 1 Corinthians 12:13—The Holy Spirit baptizes (literally, "immerses") us into the body of Christ.

1. Read Galatians 3:26–27 and Romans 6:3, noting that the scripture says that when we come to faith we are baptized into Christ's body.
   a. Read John 3:5 and note that the rebirth is of the water and the Spirit.
   b. Read again Acts 2:47 and notice that it was *the Lord* that added to their number (the church body).

    c. Why do you think that it is critical that a person knows that Christ, working through the Holy Spirit, is the one who adds us to the body and that it is not an act of our own righteousness or self-will, that is, "joining the church"?

2. What does it mean to be baptized (immersed) into something?

3. Why might it be argued that an individual is not completely surrendered to Christ, if not connected and involved in his body?

4. Jesus implemented what we call the "Lord's Supper" during his last Passover meal with the apostles (Luke 22:14–20; Matt. 26:26–29; Mark 14:22–25).
   a. The Lord's Supper is the communion meal of the body of Christ.
   b. Paul said that in partaking of it, we must recognize the church as the body of Christ and that the failure to do so could result in dire consequences (1 Cor. 11:27–29). What does he say these consequences might be?

   c. Why do you think this communion meal, also sometimes called the "Eucharist" (meaning "thanksgiving"), is a critical element in the life of the church body?

   d. The early church seems to have been participating in the Lord's Supper weekly if not even daily. Why do you believe such frequency was so important to them in comparison to the infrequent participation of many churches today?

5. In Ephesians 2:14, the apostle Paul says that Jesus is our "peace" in the body of Christ. In Ephesians 4:3, Paul calls him the "bond of peace" and says that we should make every effort to maintain the unity the Spirit gives us through the bond of peace (Jesus). Thus why must every Christian take the body of Christ very seriously?

Further Study

1. Read Rom 8:1–4. Paul says there is no condemnation for those who are *in* Christ (or the body of Christ). Why do you think that is the case? You might also consider John 15:1–8 in regard to this.
   _____
   _____
   _____

2. Read Romans 8:14–17. Paul says that it is those who are led by the Spirit that are children of God. As children we are coheirs of our Father's inheritance. Who is it, then, that brings us into Christ, makes us God's children, and unites us to one another as a family of the children of God?
   _____
   _____
   _____

Key Scripture: 1 Peter 2:9–17—The body of Christ is on a mission.

1. God designed the church with a special mission and purpose. Over the centuries the church at large (and as individual denominations and congregations as well) has sometimes clearly lost sight of this. Why do you suppose this has happened?
   _____
   _____

2. What words does the apostle Peter use to describe the church?
   _____
   _____

3. In these verses, what does he specifically say the church's purpose is in this world—what we were called out to do (verse 9)?
   _____
   _____

4. In verses 11–17, what specific instructions does he give to the church about living out its purpose?
   _____
   _____
   _____

Further Study

1. Read Eph. 4:11–16. Why does Paul say Jesus appointed these certain kinds of leaders?
   _____
   _____
   _____

2. What are the implications to you and every member?

   _____
   _____
   _____

3. Find the definitions of each of these leadership roles in this particular context. If you have not already become acquainted with them, there are plenty of excellent books and online resources for understanding scripture. If you need help, a pastor or another mature disciple will gladly help you navigate your way to them.

   a. Apostles:
      _____
      _____
      _____

   b. Prophets:
      _____
      _____
      _____

   c. Evangelists:
      _____
      _____
      _____

   d. Pastors:
      _____
      _____
      _____

   e. Teachers:
      _____
      _____
      _____

4. In 2 Corinthians 5:16–21, the apostle Paul says we are Christ's ambassadors in the world. What are the implications of that role as given in this text?

   _____
   _____
   _____

Key Scripture: Romans 12:4–8—God gives each of us gifts to use in serving the body.

1. In Christ, all the members together constitute one body in which Christ dwells. As disciples there are certain responsibilities and gifts we are all generally given. We are all then expected to utilize these gifts of discipleship. We also have all been given special gifts to contribute to the common good of the body. What are some talents in which certain individuals may be especially gifted to serve the body and other members?

   _____
   _____
   _____

2. It is the responsibility of every member to be involved in "building up the body." Consider a few of the commands for each member in building up the body. These are often called "one another" verses because they instruct us on things we should do to and for one another. Briefly summarize the command(s) after each scripture.

   a. Romans 12:10

   b. John 13:14

   c. John 13:34

   d. 1 Corinthians 12:25

   e. Galatians 5:13

   f. Ephesians 5:21

   g. Hebrews 3:13

   h. Hebrews 10:25

   i. James 5:16

j. 1 Peter 3:8

k. 1 Peter 4:9–10

3. Given the magnitude and scope of all the commands that we are each given, what conclusions must be reached concerning the way a Christian functions and participates in a local church community, especially regarding how we are to serve and treat one another?

4. Which of the commands could a Christian not carry out effectively without being an intimate part of a community?

5. What does it say about someone who does not want to be or try to be a part of a local church family?

6. How do you see these commands applying to you in both obeying them and allowing others to do them for or to you?

7. Given these commands, what characteristics should one look for in selecting a church family?

Self-Reflection

1. Describe the body of Christ.

2. Why is it vital for me to be an involved, active part of the body of Christ?

3. Since it is Christ who is building his church, how will following him as a deeply devoted disciple allow him to "build" me into the body of Christ?

4. Reviewing the scriptures above, what are some specific things that I need to do in regard to the body of Christ?

5. Do I feel able and empowered in the church I am currently in to obey the Bible's commands in regard to how to treat and minister to other Christians? And if not, what steps might I take to remedy the matter?

LESSON 12
Living as a Christian

Introduction

This is how we know we are in him: Whoever claims to live in him must live as Jesus did. (John the Apostle, 1 John 2:5–6)

GOD SAID, "BE HOLY, AS I AM HOLY." Peter calls us "a holy nation" and a people "belonging to God." To discover Jesus is to discover holiness. Living as a Christian means to live a life that is set apart. "Holy" means to be set apart for God's use alone. Jesus said, "Those of you who do not give up everything you have cannot be my disciples" (Luke 14:33). Paul said, "You are not your own; you were bought at a price" (1 Cor. 6:19–20) and, "He [Jesus] died for all, that those who live should no longer live for themselves but for him who died for them and was raised again" (2 Cor. 5:15).

Jesus said the road to life was narrow and only a few would find it. And sadly, Jesus said the majority would go to destruction (Matt. 7:13–14). It is easy to get the *glory of God* confused with the *grace of God*. The fact that God is immeasurably graceful in no way absolves us from giving our best in order to be like the best, Jesus Christ, in all his glory. God's goodness and grace frees us from guilt and the burden of sin so that we can pursue God with freedom and confidence. Peter said, "His [Christ's] divine power has given us everything we need for a godly life through our knowledge of him who called us by his own glory and goodness" (2 Pet. 1:3). We are called *by* his glory and goodness *to* his glory and goodness. Paul said of himself, "I have [not] already obtained all this, or have already arrived at my goal, but I press on to take hold of that for which Christ Jesus took hold of me" (Phil. 3:13).

The reality is that one cannot follow Christ (be a disciple) and live haphazardly or carelessly. The Christian life is a purposeful life. It is a life of living like Jesus. However, many, in their quests to preach pure gospel, have inadvertently called others to accept Christ as their savior and not taught them to accept him as their Lord. Thus many Christians scarcely look and live like Jesus and would likely not even be able to describe adequately what Jesus was like. If one "accepts the gospel" with a sense of entitlement to Christ rather than in a sense of indebtedness to him, the Christian life to follow will be a self-serving one. Such a life will be lived based on self—what "I want," what "I like," and what makes me "feel good." Rarely does one start out wrong and end up right, especially in the highest endeavor of all—that of following Christ!

Christian churches, too full of self-serving Christians, easily take on the look and feel of modern businesses or retail outlets, striving for top "customer service" and entertainment value. Churches compete for members based on services offered or amenities available. Members are treated as customers rather than as "employees," let alone as servants. They are treated as guests rather than the hosts they are called to be. Members are served rather than being expected to serve. Members too often behave as spoiled, cranky customers shopping for just the "right" thing, and if that thing is not found quickly, then running off to the next church. Jokes can easily be heard about the rude behavior of church members out in the parking lots after church services, racing each other to the most popular nearby restaurants. Churches will never be better than their leaders call them to be. Members will never be better than their leaders teach, live their lives, and expect members to live their own lives. A church will never be better than its members.

Christ lived a selfless life. Christ came to give everything. Christ came to serve everyone. Christ came to die for all. How then can one live a selfish life, especially a selfish Christian life, and lay claim to being a follower of him? The purpose of this lesson is to look at the Christian life through Jesus's foundational teachings in the Sermon on the Mount. Combining this lesson with Lesson 7, "Following Jesus," should provide a new or a renewed Christian at least a solid template for walking as Jesus did.

Key Lesson: Developing the character of Christ.

1. Matthew seems to have recorded Jesus's primary teachings and eventually wrote them in his gospel of Jesus. In Matthew 5–7, he records the most complete account of what has come to be known as the Sermon on the Mount. This is because Matthew starts this chapter saying that Jesus went up on a mount and began to teach them. The Sermon on the Mount seems impossible to follow for many. The teachings are not about receiving the grace of God. The teachings are about giving grace to others. The Sermon is about graceful living. Because Jesus lived gracefully, his followers will live gracefully. That's what Christian living is about.

2. Read Matthew 5:1–12. These statements are known as the "beatitudes." "Beatitude" means "a supreme blessing." Possessing the character trait mentioned brings the supreme blessing associated with it. Our goal, our aim, as Christians is to be just like God. And God is perfect. Jesus in fact commanded us to be perfect as God is perfect (Matt. 5:48). The word used for "sin" in the New Testament is the Greek word *hamartia*, which means "to miss the mark." We miss the "mark" of God in our aim to be like him by "falling short of his glory" (Rom. 3:23). We are forgiven of that failure when we accept the saving work of Christ in our lives so that God sees us as being perfect (Eph. 1:4; Rom. 8:1–4). But Christ teaches us to make our aim to be perfect just as God is perfect. He searches our hearts, and he knows what our real aim is—whether it is to strive for Christ's perfection and be justified by his sacrifice, or it is to justify our own less-than-perfect behavior under the excuse that "nobody is perfect."

3. Developing the character of Christ and participating in the divine nature of God is our design as image bearers, and it is in fact our calling. Our personal responsibility is to come to know—to focus our minds and our hearts on—and to obey Jesus (2 Cor. 3:18; Heb. 3:1; 1 John 2:3–6). In doing that, the Holy Spirit transforms us so that we grow in possessing the character of Christ in increasing measure. And this brings a "supreme blessedness."

4. Consider each Christlike attribute he promises to bless. Note the specific blessing corresponding to each of these qualities we are to grow in. In the space provided, note how you think each of these blessings relates to the specific quality they are attached to, and then how you personally need to grow in regard to it.
    a. Poor in spirit = the opposite of "full of yourself" or of self-centeredness; being empty of selfish ambition and self-interest (2 Cor. 8:9; Phil. 2:5–8; 2 Cor. 5:14–15)
        i. The blessing: given the kingdom of heaven = acceptance into God's kingdom

ii. What is the relation of the trait to blessing?
_____
_____
_____

iii. Personal growth opportunity?
_____
_____
_____

b. Mourning = being sensitized to the world as God sees it; the opposite of "apathetic" (Isa. 53:1–3; Heb. 5:7; James 4:7–10; 2 Cor. 7:10–11)
   i. The blessing: being comforted, receiving the only real comfort that exists amid the pains and frustrations of the world
   ii. Relation of trait to blessing?
   _____
   _____
   _____

   iii. Personal growth opportunity?
   _____
   _____
   _____

c. Meek = humble and restrained of heart; harnessed for God's purposes (Matt. 11:28–29; Mark 10:42–44; James 4:10)
   i. The blessing: inherit the earth = be heirs of God
   ii. Relation of trait to blessing?
   _____
   _____
   _____

   iii. Personal growth opportunity?
   _____
   _____

d. Hungering and thirsting for righteousness = a healthy desire for, more than anything else, a "right relationship" with God; a deep inner desire to live rightly, through God's power and grace, in his perfection and goodness (1 Pet. 2:2; Psa. 42:1; Luke 5:16; John 5:19; 14:31)
   i. The blessing: filled = receive the spiritual food that is truly food
   ii. Relation of trait to blessing?
   _____
   _____
   _____

   iii. Personal growth opportunity?
   _____
   _____
   _____

e. Being merciful = kind, compassionate, understanding, and forgiving (Luke 6:27–36; Matt. 9:12-13; Col. 3:12–14)
   i. The blessing: shown mercy = receive the kindness, compassion, and forgiveness of God
   ii. Relation of trait to blessing?
   _____
   _____
   _____

   iii. Personal growth opportunity?
   _____
   _____
   _____

f. Pure in heart = a singleness of heart, mind, and life that is focused foremost on God and has no place for rivals to him; without ungodly contamination (Psa. 24:3–4; 51:10; John 8:12, 46; Matt. 23:25–26; 1 Tim. 1:5)
   i. The blessing: seeing God = experiencing God in a most real and experiential way
   ii. Relation of trait to blessing?
   _____
   _____
   _____

   iii. Personal growth opportunity?
   _____
   _____
   _____

g. Being a peacemaker = at peace with God and man through humility, surrender, self-sacrifice, and evangelism, living to lead others in coming to such a peace (Rom. 12:14–19; Isa. 9:6; Col. 3:15; Eph. 2:14–15; James 3:17)
   i. The blessing: called children of God = be identified with the firstborn of the sons of God, Jesus Christ
   ii. Relation of trait to blessing?
   _____
   _____
   _____

   iii. Personal growth opportunity?
   _____
   _____
   _____

h. Persecuted = living as a foreigner in this world, in all its darkness and evil; often results in rejection, mistreatment, injustice, ridicule, and even execution, but leads into the kingdom of God (2 Cor. 4:11; Phil. 1:29–30; 3:10–11; Heb. 11:13–16; 12:1–3)
   i. The blessing: the kingdom of heaven = to be drawn into and included in the kingdom of God

ii. Relation of trait to blessing?

iii. Personal growth opportunity?

5. Write out for yourself 2 Corinthians 3:18 in the space provided.

   a. Your work is to "behold his glory." How will you do this?

   b. God's work is to, transform you "into his likeness with ever increasing glory." What is your role in this?

   c. The requirement here is "surrender." The whole New Testament speaks the language of surrender—deny yourself, take up your cross daily, follow, serve, go, offer, give generously, give expecting nothing in return, offer your bodies as living sacrifices, live no longer for yourselves, go the extra mile, lay down your life, be the least, be the worst, be the last, give up everything you have, and so forth. Given the completeness of surrender that is required to live as a Christian as Christ wants us to, what is the difference between attempting to be transformed by your own efforts and strength and surrendering to God's transforming power seen in Jesus, and when, on the outside, it may initially look just the same?

Key Lesson: Developing the influence of Christ.

1. Read Matthew 5:13–16. Consider the effects of salt and of light, as the original hearers would have understood. In other words, they had no way to understand the science behind light and salt, but they only saw their presence and their effects. What will it look like in our lives as Christians to be both "salt" and "light" in this world—what does their presence "look like" and what are their effects?

2. Consider next a bit of the science behind salt and light.
    a. Salt preserves food. It does this by literally drawing the water out of microbes or molds through osmosis and thus killing them. How do you see that devoted Christians can similarly "suck the life out of" the evil which attacks the world around us?

    b. Salt also seasons. It makes foods taste better in a number of ways. It brings out or enhances other flavors. What are some ways we as Christians can enhance the world or make it "taste better"?

    c. Light energizes. Sunlight provides the energy the living ecosystems of earth need to exist. God is the light that provides the energy for the whole universe to sustain itself and continue. How do we as Christians serve as conduits of the light of God, providing energy for a dying world?

    d. Light enlightens. Light can show the truth of what is around us and what is going on. Science is still trying to figure light out. Much is known; much is to be learned. In a very simplistic explanation, objects are made visible to our eye receptors when a wave of light strikes an object before us. The photons in that light energize the surface atoms of the object, which in turn causes electrons in them to move to a higher orbit. In doing so photons of light are emitted. That's what we see. The light of Christ does the same to us. It strikes us, energizes us, and causes us to light up in the world around us. This light reveals the truth to us, and causes light to be emitted from us. This light shows God for who he is, and it also lights up the world around us in both its beautiful and its dire realities. Think of ways that we as Christians are to be lights of the world, enlightening others to the truths of God?

    e. Light guides. In our modern, often overly lighted world, the metaphors of a city on a hill and of candles on a stand are not very impacting. But during Jesus's time, for the traveler caught out in the wilderness at night and not knowing where to go and how to get there, lights from a town on a hill would be most welcome sights. And a candle or lamp on the floor, or worse under a dark shade, will not provide much light for a room. Lights placed high in a room will light a much larger area. How can we be lights in the world and position ourselves up high in order to guide others, provide hope to the lost and the hurting, and to otherwise light a much larger area around us with the truth of God?

3. How does the idea of being salt and light in the world connect with our Christian mission of seeking and saving the lost?

4. How might you need to grow in being salt and light in the world around you?

5. List some ways you believe Christians are lights to the world, as light was described earlier.

6. List some ways you believe we are to be the salt of the earth, as salt was described above.

Further Study

1. Consider some other passages concerning Christians and salt, and make a note about what is likely meant by each.
    a. Luke 14:34–35

    b. Mark 9:50

    c. Colossians 4:6

    d. Leviticus 2:13

2. Note some passages concerning Christians and light, and make notes of what each likely is talking about.
    a. Ephesians 5:8

b. John 8:12

c. 1 John 1:5–7

d. Philippians 2:15–16

e. Romans 13:11–14

Key Lesson: Developing the attitude of Christ

1. Read Matthew 5:21–42 to consider these particular attitudes Christ is calling us to. Then consider a bit of preliminary information first.
2. Some introductory information is necessary to understand Jesus's statements in this text.
   a. Jesus from the very beginning of his ministry spoke with an authority unseen by Israel. Read Mark 1:21–28 and Matthew 7:28–29.
      1) In Mark 1:22, 27, what were the people so amazed about?

      2) Who did they contrast his teaching with (verse 21)?

      3) Why do you think Jesus's casting out of the demon showed to them his authority?

   b. To the Jews the Law of Moses was the absolute and final authority. The law was considered itself as divine.
      1) The law in many ways WAS God to them (remember why humankind chose the Tree of Knowledge of Good and Evil).
      2) The synagogues were similar to our modern churches and church buildings. The Jews gathered in these for their worship. The opening of synagogue worship was the taking of the scroll of the Law from the ark (a box) and marching it around so that the worshipers could show reverence

to it. Do you see a similar response sometimes to the Bible itself? If so, how so, and what is the danger of doing such?

_____
_____
_____

c. Refer again to Matthew 5:21–42. Note that five times in this text alone, Jesus quotes the Law only to amend it (Matthew 5:21, 27, 33, 38, 43).
   1) What do you notice about what Jesus was adding to each of the Old Testament laws, or how he was actually amending them?

   _____
   _____
   _____

   2) Read Matthew 23:26. In this verse, we see that Jesus later told the Jews to clean the inside of the cup and the outside would be clean. How does this relate to what Jesus added to each of the old laws?

   _____
   _____
   _____

   3) Why are we so prone to clean the outside of our lives and leave the inside of our hearts dirty?

   _____
   _____
   _____

d. The Greek word for authority (*exousia*) used in this text means "the power to add and the power to take away at will."
   1) Read Deuteronomy 12:32 and Revelations 22:18–19. Moses, concerning the Law, says no one is to add to or take from it. Also at the end of the very last book of the Bible, Jesus clearly warns that no one has the right to add to or take from his final messages. Only God can give such laws, and only God can amend his laws. In the Sermon on the Mount, Jesus himself was clearly adding to the each of these laws of Moses. What does that say about Jesus's authority and who he is?

   _____
   _____

   2) Jesus taught not just as one *with* authority; Jesus says he *is* the final authority (note also Matt. 28:18)! How are these two expressions different?

   _____
   _____

   3) Read Matthew 12:8. Arguably, the Jews considered the Sabbath to be the most holy expression of their relationship with God. The Sabbath observance was established as one of the Ten Commandments. Practicing Jews still consider it as their most important regular religious observance. God established the Sabbath Day. Matthew tells us a story in Matthew 12:8 in which Jesus concludes it, telling the Jews he was, in fact, "Lord of the Sabbath."

a) Who would the Jews have considered at that point to be the Lord of the Sabbath?
___
___

b) What then was Jesus telling them in saying that he was Lord of the Sabbath (John 5:18)?
___
___

e. Even the prophets of old had never claimed the authority to speak as authoritatively as Jesus did. They began their sayings with, "Thus saith the Lord…" (KJV) or, depending on the translation you are reading, something similar to, "the Lord says…" (although there are many, for example, Ezek. 13: 3 and Jer. 23:16). They were not appealing to their own authority but only to God's. How does this differ from the way Jesus spoke in the Sermon on the Mount?
___
___
___

f. Further down the line, the Jewish rabbis and teachers would say, as they began speaking on a topic, something such as, "There is a teaching that says…" Again, they were not appealing to their own authority but to the authority of the Law itself, or at least to one of their handed-down traditions or interpretations of the Law. How does this differ from the way Jesus spoke in the Sermon on the Mount?
___
___

g. The Jews revered the Law of Moses as we revere Jesus. They believed their relationship with God was based on the Law of Moses plus *nothing else*, just as we believe we are saved by the work of Christ plus *nothing else*! In that regard, note how Jesus opens his teachings, "But I tell you…"! Jesus speaks and acts as if he was his own authority. He does not refer to God ("thus saith the Lord") or the Law of Moses ("a teaching says"). Near the end of his life, he would later tell the apostles plainly, "If you have seen me, you have seen the Father" (John 14:9). What does this tell us about Jesus's authority to make laws and take laws away?
___
___
___

h. The reality is that Jesus calls them to only one of a few choices concerning his identity. Why do you in your own beliefs personally choose or reject each of these?
1) He had final authority.
___
___
___

2) He had a demon.
___
___
___

3) He was crazy.

4) He was brazen and evil.

i. In Capernaum an impure spirit in a member of the synagogue recognized Jesus, as was to happen over and over with the evil spirits. These impure spirits are often called demons or unclean spirits. The demons in fact recognized in Jesus what the closed Jewish minds most often could not. These Jews were still in fact full of the fruit of the Tree of the Knowledge of Good and Evil. Their faith was in their own righteousness and national membership rather than in God. What does it perhaps infer that an impure spirit inhabited one of their members?

1) Not only was Jesus's authority staggering to the Jews; his teaching was staggering to them. What amazed them about his teaching?

   a) The Jews, as do Christians today with the New Testament, often seemingly used the Old Testament as a doctrine of minimums, as if to ask the question, "what is the minimum amount I have to give or do?" How does this compare with Jesus's own doctrine concerning giving the best and the most we could (Matt. 22:37–39; Luke 14:33)?

   b) Jesus clearly usurped their interpretation and application of the Law in its minimum standards with God's original intention for them in regard to the Law—giving the best and the most. When asked by the teachers of the law what was the greatest commandment of the Law, Jesus summarized their whole law with, "love God with ALL of you heart, soul and mind" (Matt. 22:35–37; Deut. 6:5). The first four of the Ten Commandments have to do with loving God. How does this view of giving your all change the whole interpretation of the Law, or any law for that matter?

   c) The teachers of the law in the last verse above did not ask for a second commandment, but Jesus gives them one anyway, "love your neighbor as yourself." He was quoting Leviticus

19:18. The last six of the Ten Commandments have to do with how we treat each other. What does this tell us is the overarching intent of the last six of the Commandments?

_____
_____
_____

j. In this lifetime, we will never fully understand the depths of the teachings of Jesus's Sermon on the Mount, because this is in actuality God talking, and thus these truths are rooted in his very nature, which we cannot grasp or "see" in this present age, and perhaps not in the next. Consider what Moses said in Deuteronomy 29:29. Although we can never understand God completely, and thus we can never understand all of the implications of his words, what are we to do, as best we can, with what he *has* revealed to us?

_____
_____
_____

k. Consider the concentric rings of biblical interpretation discussed in Lesson 2 from outer to inner: people, culture, religion, and God. In studying scripture, we must peel off the husk to see the essence of God ultimately found in Jesus. Jesus said to the Jews (John 5:39–40) that they were looking at scriptures but they were not finding God. How do you think this is possible?

_____
_____
_____

l. In the Sermon on the Mount, Jesus sets the highest standard possible—God's perfection. Read Matthew 5:48.
   1) What is our responsibility as to our efforts in seeking to be like God?

   _____
   _____
   _____

   2) Considering Ephesians 1:4, how does God see us from the time we become Christians?

   _____
   _____
   _____

3. Consider each of the teachings (Matt. 5:21–42) of Jesus concerning how to think and act toward others. Make a note after each how you think you can grow in regard to, or apply in life, each of these principles.
   a. Read verses 21–22. Not only must we not murder another, we must restrain our anger and any condemning attitudes toward others. In the New Testament there are two kinds of anger. One is the quick-burn kind where something makes us angry but it goes away quickly. The other is the slow-burn kind. This is when anger turns into bitterness. This is the kind of anger Jesus is speaking of here. What Jesus seems to be indicating is that to him, when we choose the route of this kind of long-term and seething bitterness, we are going down the path that ultimately leads to harming others or even to murder. But it constitutes murdering others in our own hearts. It brings us into judgment of the

first degree—being liable to the village court. This was the local court of a village itself. It is not the biggest deal, but it is still a deal. To God at least. Have you ever felt, or do you now, feel this kind of anger toward anyone else?

___

b. The term "raca" is a term of contempt that was used to say someone was intellectually stupid. We must not intellectually condemn others whom God has also created (as if to say they are "stupid"). This, he says, brings judgment to a higher degree—to the Sanhedrin, their national court. Why is this worse than simply retaining anger toward another?

___

c. How does this occur in and around you?

___

d. The third degree he mentions is calling someone a fool. Here Jesus is speaking of calling someone morally useless—completely without worth, and it deserves the greatest punishment. *Gahenna* is the term Jesus used. It refers to the smoldering place in Jerusalem where garbage was burned, and it became a symbol of hell itself. To call another useless is to become useless yourself, it seems. How have you felt this or seen this occur in the world around us?

___

e. Christians must value others as God values them. Christians imitating Christ must love others as Christ loves them. Christians must look with love on even the most despised and hated of the world. We must be the love of Christ to these that the world may marginalize and cast away. How do you see yourself in this regard?

___

f. How can we, however, be realistic in the way we regard others without being condemning of them?

___

g. Can we somehow not despise and condemn others who may otherwise squander their lives and do evil and still not condone their actions and lives, and if so, how?

___

h. Note verses 23–24, and for further reference read Ephesians 4:26–32. We should make reconciling relationships with others a priority, even before offering our worship to God. In this case, Jesus speaks of our coming to worship and pray to God and then realize or remember someone else has something against us. The Jews would take their offerings they wanted to sacrifice to God to the temple and hand it over a rail to one of the awaiting priests, who were the ones that actually made the offerings on the altar. Jesus said in this case to leave your gift there at the rail, and go try to make right whatever the other is holding against you. Why do you suppose it is important to God that before we come to worship him that we take the responsibility for, and thus take the initiative to clear up, others' offenses against us?

i. Do you currently know of anyone who might be holding an offense against you that, if at all possible, you might need to try to settle up with?

j. Read verses 25–26. We should settle matters quickly with our adversaries as well. In this text, Jesus is obviously referring to a debt of some kind that we owe to another ("you will not get out until you have paid the last penny"). Jesus wants us to be "agreeable" people rather than "disagreeable" people. Jesus says his followers should not be the ones to try to "get the best" of others. And in a principle that has been worded variously over the years, morals and ethics are not about rights but about right. They are not about what we *can* do but about what we *should* do. What applications do you see for yourself concerning this principle?

k. Consider verses 27–28. We should check not only our adulterous behaviors; we should also keep our thoughts about sin in check. The penalty for adultery was to be death (Lev. 20:10). The law against adultery is first given in the seventh of the Ten Commandments. The tenth of the Commandments was not to covet (or lust). The word used for "covet" or "lust" means "to long after with great desire." This is not simply an evil desire. James describes our descent in to sin as beginning with being enticed by our own evil desire. It is then that evil desire conceives and gives birth to sin. When sin grows up, it brings death (James 1:14–15). James is using the illustration of human procreation. In it, there is desire, intimacy, conception, gestation, birth, and development. At what point do you think sexual attraction for another actually becomes sinful?

l. Have you ever committed adultery in actuality or in your heart? (However, consider carefully the wisdom of what you actually write down here in this regard.) If the answer is "yes" though, it would be wise to speak to a minister, pastor, counselor, or spiritually mature friend for confession, any corrections that need to be made, and healing.
    _____
    _____

m. Give some examples of how our evil sexual desires can become sinful, and also how our evil desires for other kinds of things can become sinful (consider the tenth Commandment, Exod. 20:17).
    _____
    _____

n. Read verses 29 and 30 carefully. Jesus suggests a radical, surgical cure for destructive sin. In this text, the word used concerning the cause for stumbling is the one that refers to the stick or arm that the bait was attached to in an animal trap. When the animal took the bait, it was caught. It was a word then used for anything that caused a man to be trapped or destroyed. Jesus is talking about the objects of our own evil desires that are bait for us but that are in traps just waiting for us. Behind these desires are the perils that will cause our undoing. As with animals, each of us may have our own specific desires that can be used as bait to trap us. This bait draws us down a dangerous path where our predators either set something stealthily in our paths, such as stone or a trip wire, or dig a pit and carefully cover it with sticks and leaves. One will trip us and allow us to be attacked. The other will trap us and put us in a hole. What it is that draws us down the wrong path, however, is the bait. Consider 1 John 2:16. John describes the things that come from the world as the lust of the flesh, the lust of the eyes, and the pride of life (see these three lusts in the original sin, Genesis 3:6—good for food, pleasing to the eye, and making one "like God"). In this regard, consider your own lust preferences.

    1) What is it that tempts your eyes? Forbidden sexual things? Greed of money and material things? Prideful or selfish life situations?
        _____
        _____

    2) What is it that tempts your ears? Gossip? Evil music, videos, and movies? Sexualized, sensual conversations and talk? Divisive, factious talk?
        _____
        _____

    3) What tempts your tastes? Illegal drugs or improperly used prescription drugs? Drunkenness? Binge eating? Laziness? Overspending? Overindulgent gambling or sports?
        _____
        _____
        _____

4) What tempts your sinful pride? Feeling better than others in looks, intelligence, popularity, sports, or just being cool? Houses, cars, and wealth?

_____

5) Although the most radical and literal interpretation of cutting off limbs and gouging out eyes would certainly be more desirable than eternal destruction, Jesus is surely not advocating self-mutilation, but rather is talking about decisive and incisive actions we must take to root out the evil desires that lead us into life's destructive traps. What might need to be rooted out of your own life?

_____

6) Who might best be able to help you with this? Make a plan.

_____

o. Note verses 31–32. Divorce should be taken most seriously, and we should not be looking for an excuse to divorce, but instead we need to search for ways to preserve and protect our marriage covenants.
   1) There were three cultures that influenced the Christians of this time: Jewish, Greek, and Roman.
      a) The Jews had originally been given a most godly and lofty view of marriage through the Law of Moses. A man was ever only to delay or abstain from marriage in order to devote himself wholly to the study of the Torah. The Jews believed the command to "be fruitful and multiply," that is to bear offspring, to be a sacred command to all men. And further the Jews ideally were to hate divorce. It was God who said through the prophet Malachi, "I hate divorce" (Mal. 2:16). As with many others of God's laws, the Jews had institutionalized the constant violation of the intent of God's marital law, which was meant to create a sacred bond. Instead of a wife being seen by a man as a precious blessing from God, women were treated as property. Men could easily divorce a woman for any reason; however, under the male-domination curse (Gen. 3:16), women could only be divorced with his approval. How does the Bible intend for men/husbands to treat women/wives (1 Pet. 3:7), and how does the Bible intend for women/wives to treat men, as well as each other for that matter (Eph. 5:21)?

_____

      b) The Greek culture, which had permeated most of the Roman Empire by Jesus's time, saw marriage as the means to have children and have a wife to run the house. For men of means, concubines were for daily cohabitation. Prostitutes were for the pleasure of all men. The inherit adulteration of marriage was systemic to the Hellenistic culture. How do you see similarities to our modern culture?

_____

    c) The Romans had begun their history with a more noble view of marriage but seemingly had been corrupted by the baser Greek views.
  2) In Matthew 19:1–12, Matthew tells us the Jews asked Jesus if they were allowed to divorce for any reason. Summarize Jesus's answer to them.

  3) Why does it follow that if a married man and woman are being transformed into the character and attitudes of Christ, as seen in the first part of Matthew 5, that divorce is not only completely avoidable, but that a good marriage is inevitable?

 p. Read verses 33–37. Our word should be our final word. We should not have to make oaths and swear beyond a simple "yes" or "no." Jesus is the truth personified, and he wants us to "be the truth as well." If one is truthful, one will by definition tell the truth. How honest is our society today, and how honest and trustworthy are you?

 q. Note verses 38–42. Christians should not be seekers of revenge, as that is God's role. We should not even be most concerned with our "rights" or what is "fair" for us. Our concern should be what God is concerned about. We take care of his business; he takes care of our business. We should avoid fights and be extra generous to those that would use us. How do you feel our society looks at this, and how do you look at this?

4. Matthew was writing a gospel to Jewish Christians and other Jews that might read his book. Quoting the teachings of Jesus, he takes extra effort to correct their wrong interpretations of their written law and the oral traditions they had created to interpret it. How do you see that their flawed attitudes led to these flawed applications of the law?

5. Do you think some of the same problems of interpretation of the New Testament may have swept over the Christian church in the two thousand years of its existence?

6. How do you think we can personally avoid that same trap of allowing incorrect or bad attitudes about truth to lead to incorrect applications of truth?

Further Study

1. Read the following scriptures, and consider how each helps better understand God's views and instructions on the principles discussed above.
   a. Anger and bitterness
      i. Ephesians 4:26–31

      ii. James 1:19–20

      iii. Proverbs 29:11

      iv. Colossians 3:8

   b. Condemning others
      i. Proverbs 19:11

      ii. James 4:1–3

      iii. James 4:11–12

      iv. 1 John 3:11–12

- c. Reconciliation and peace
  - i. Romans 12:17–21

  - ii. Matthew 18:15–17

  - iii. 1 Peter 4:8

  - iv. Galatians 5:13–15

- d. Adultery and failure to keep our covenants and our word
  - i. Ecclesiastes 5:4–6

  - ii. Matthew 19:9

  - iii. Hebrews 13:4

  - iv. Malachi 2:10–16

  - v. Proverbs 2:16–19

vi. James 4:4–10

2. Read Matthew 15:10–20 and 23:26. What does Jesus say must happen in order to change these bad attitudes he speaks of?

Key Lesson: Developing the love of Christ.

1. Read Matthew 5:43–48. Consider the points Jesus makes about loving like God loves, and how each contrasts with worldly love and how you might apply each in your own life.
   a. Love your enemies.

   b. Pray for those who persecute you.

   c. Just as God blesses his enemies so should we.

   d. In fact, when we merely love those who love us, we are still no different than unconverted unbelievers.

   e. God is perfect love, and we should strive to imitate his perfect love (1 John 4:7–12).

2. How is the love of Christ not only different from worldly love but also far superior to and different from even what is often seen among Christians?

Key Lesson: Developing the life of Christ.

1. Read Matthew 6:1–24. Christ, it may be said, "walked the walk." He came to the earth and began by showing the people of Israel how to live even before he began to teach them. Under each point, write out how Jesus wants us to think or behave as seen in this text.
   a. When giving to the needy.
   _____
   _____
   _____

   b. In public prayer.
   _____
   _____
   _____

   c. In private or public prayer.
   _____
   _____
   _____

   d. In fasting.
   _____
   _____
   _____

2. Jesus assumes his followers will be generous to the needy and faithful in prayer, as well as engage in focused spiritual times of fasting and prayer. Oddly these can be three of the more neglected parts of many Christians' lives. For a discussion of "true" fasting, read Isaiah 58. The New Testament never directly explains fasting but only reveals its presence and the expectation of it, thus it must be understood by a biblical construct from the various passages where it is mentioned. However, suffice it to say, fasting is a limited time of depriving oneself of some need, such as food, in order to demonstrate one's heart desire before God and to focus oneself in on God and the need or situation being prayed over. Why do you suppose these three, and especially fasting, are often neglected?
   _____
   _____
   _____

3. How can you grow in regard to these principles?
   _____
   _____
   _____

Key Lesson: Developing the priority of Christ.

1. Read Matthew 6:19–34. Jesus summarizes this section by saying to seek first the kingdom and we will be provided all we need to live. Notice the points he makes at the beginning of this section.
   a. Our heart follows where we invest our treasure, thus we need to invest in the spiritual and eternal things (verses 19–21).

i. How can we as Christians invest in heavenly things and avoid the trap of heavily investing in the world (Col. 3:1–2)?

b. We must keep our spiritual vision clear and unobstructed by worldly priorities, lest we walk back into the darkness (verses 22–23).
   i. How can we maintain healthy spiritual vision (Heb. 3:1)?

c. We must choose whether we will serve the material world (money) or whether we will serve God, because we cannot serve both (verse 24).
   i. Why is it impossible to serve God when we live our lives for money and worldly material wealth (James 4:4)?

2. Worry and anxiety are major roadblocks to serving Christ effectively and are in fact signs of an immature, wavering, or weak faith in God (there is also a physiological basis for some kinds anxiety, which is a completely different subject than this). What point is Jesus making on each of these topics, and what argument does he make against each?
   a. Worry about life—what we will eat, drink, or wear (verses 25–26).

   b. Worry is senseless and useless (verse 27).

   c. Worrying about the clothes we wear is also foolish (verse 28).

   d. When we worry about having the basic things we need to live, whom are we behaving like (verses 31–32)?

   e. Where should our real priority be (verses 33–34)?

3. How might you need to grow in regard to worry and kingdom priorities?

___

Key Lesson: Developing the relationships of Christ.

1. Read Matthew 7:1–6, 12. In the world, we pick friendships by whom we like and whom we benefit most from, either socially or even materially. We look to see what is in it for us in any relationship we might be considering forming. Christ again and again teaches a new attitude toward relationships.
   a. Do not judge. The type of judgment spoken of in this text is condemnation and harsh criticism. It is the kind of judgment that shows an unwillingness to bear with others and usually demands more than it gives (verse 1). What is the difference between the evaluations and constructive criticisms, we are in some instances commanded to give to each other, that we might receive from a parent, a pastor, a mentor, or a teacher, and what might be considered destructive criticism, judgment, or condemnation? (As you consider the answer to this question, read these scriptures: 1 Cor. 5:12; 2 Tim. 4:2; John 7:24; and Col. 3:15–16. They qualify that in some instances Christians must make certain kinds of "judgments.")

   ___

   b. You will, however, be judged in the same way you judge (verse 2). Why do you believe this is the case, both with God's judgment of you and with other people's judgments of you?

   ___

   c. We must first clear the debris from our own eyes in order to help clear our brother or sister's eyes (verses 3–5). What does this mean?

   ___

   d. Do not give yourself, your heart, your good message, or your good name to those who will not appreciate it and will trample on it (verse 6). How do we see this principle play out in Jesus's own life?

   ___

2. Jesus gives what is probably one of the most famous relationship principles in verse 12, usually called the "golden rule." How does this apply: should we do to people what we want done for or to us, or what they want done for or to them? Explain.

   ___

Key Lesson: Developing the focus of Christ.

1. Read Matthew 7:7–12. Jesus sought God with all of his heart, praying early and often (Mark 1:35; Luke 5:16). He was also most earnest in his obedience to God (John 14:31). Explain what you believe each of these to mean.
   a. Ask and it will be given to you.

   b. Seek and you will find.

   c. Knock and the door will be opened to you.

2. Even earthly parents give good gifts to their children; so how much more will God give to his children who ask? What sort of confidence should this give us in our relationships with our heavenly Father?

   a. How will a devoted child of God determine what to ask for, what and how to seek, and how to keep knocking on God's door, so to speak (for help, read 1 John 4:14–15)?

Key Lesson: Developing the faith of Christ.

1. Read Matthew 7:13–29. Jesus concludes the Sermon on the Mount with some very challenging principles. Although faith is not specifically even mentioned in this text, these verses breathe with the message of trusting God. To develop the character, attitude, and life of Christ requires tremendous faith in and reliance on God to transform you. You have to really trust him. Note the salient points Jesus delivers in this scripture.
   a. The broad road to destruction is the one many go down. In our natural selves, we humans feel safer when in the crowd. But Jesus says that going with the crowd is not such a good idea. He also says the

easy way is not the right way. Why do you think going with the crowd and choosing the easy way leads to destruction?
_____
_____

b. The narrow road to life is the one few go down. Why do you think few go down this road, and why does it have to be so narrow?
_____
_____

c. Any "easy, broad" way may equal wrong, but does a "hard, narrow" way necessarily equal the right way of God? Explain.
_____
_____

d. We must be wary of false prophets
   i. They look harmless. At first glance, they look like real people of God. How can we be wary of false leaders without being fearful of all leaders?
   _____
   _____

   ii. But they are definitely not harmless. Why are we so susceptible to insincere or false leaders?
   _____
   _____

   iii. False and insincere prophets and leaders can only be recognized by the fruit they bear—ultimately by the results of what they produce. Hebrews says to consider carefully the "outcome of their way of life" (Heb. 13:7).
      1. Remember it this way: false prophets lead you to them not to him (Jesus). Bad or false leaders prefer to lead followers. Godly leaders prefer to lead leaders—people who, because they are following Christ, will inherently lead/feed/shepherd others. Insincere leaders use two extreme techniques to attract unsuspecting followers: making them feel awesome—feed our pride—or making them feel awful in order to make them codependent on the leaders. They bloat followers' egos, or otherwise break them down to make them completely susceptible, deferential, and submissive. How do insincere leaders, wittingly or unwittingly, attract crowds of followers using these techniques?
      _____
      _____

      2. False prophets teach people to do "religious things" ("prophesy, drive out demons, and perform miracles," Matt. 7:22), but they do not teach them to obey God, particularly in the

character areas Jesus discusses in this Sermon. Note how verses 21–23 follow verses 15–20. This is the fruit by which we must recognize false teachers—they and their ministries are producing people who call Jesus Lord and do "Jesus-like things," but they have not truly made Jesus Lord from within. Consider how this might "look" within your heart, if you were to go down, or perhaps even have gone down, this path.

___

e. Lordship is not determined by what one says, but by what one does.
   i. Jesus's key commands are given in the Sermon on the Mount, Matthew 5–7. His commands involve character, heart, and attitude change (Matt. 23:26). God sees what goes on in our hearts and minds as our inner and life-defining behaviors, even more than seeing what we do outwardly. Consider these scriptures.
      1. Jeremiah 17:9–10. Note how God connects examining our hearts and our minds with our conduct and deeds.

      ___

      2. Hebrews 4:12–13. Notice how the Word of God judges the attitudes and thoughts of our hearts. How do you think it does that?

      ___

      3. Matthew 22:37. Jesus says the greatest commandment of the Law is to love God with our hearts and our minds. Loving with our hearts and our minds is a behavior to God; an attitudinal behavior that he examines, judges, and rewards or punishes. How are we to love God with our hearts and our minds?

      ___

   ii. False prophets will impress people and teach them to impress others. How do you think this comes about?

   ___

   iii. What are some things naïve and unwitting people might be most susceptible to being impressed over and thus perhaps deceived by?

   ___

iv. Following Christ first and foremost requires our carefully listening to God's Word—what he actually says—and not just what others may say about his Word.
   1. Read again 1 John 2:3–5. Jesus's closest disciple and friend, the apostle John, wrote this.
      a. Summarize what he says is the defining mark of one who truly knows Christ.

      b. What must one actually know before one can do the will of Christ?

      c. What do the "commands" of the Sermon on the Mount mainly deal with?

   2. Read again 2 Corinthians 3:18. We are not, on our own, able to reach our target—the perfection of God (Matt. 5:48). What is our role then in making progress toward it, according to the apostle Paul? Note Philippians 2:13–14 for help.

   3. Read again Ephesians 1:4. How does God "see" or regard us when we are living and abiding in Christ?

v. Consider Matthew 7:24–27. Why is it so foolish to hear God's Word, but not put it into practice?

   1. Read and summarize James 1:22–24.

   2. Read and summarize 1 Corinthians 4:20. What does Paul mean that the kingdom of God is not a matter of "talk"?

vi. Why is it wise to truly listen to God's Word and put it into practice?

vii. Can you think of some common examples of how Christians hear what is right to do, but then consistently fail to do it?

viii. The reward for obedience will be spiritual security. Note the two houses and their ultimate fates. How does obeying Christ, from the inside out, keep us from being destroyed when life's storms come?

ix. The cost of not doing so will spell spiritual catastrophe. How does not obeying Christ, from the inside out, make us vulnerable to be destroyed amid life's storms?

x. What are some of life's storms that should be anticipated in order to not have our "houses" destroyed by them?

f. Consider Matthew 7:28–29. The way Jesus taught, and the authority with which he taught, took aback these Jews who were the first to learn from Christ. Why do you think his teaching was so different than that of their teachers of the law?

Self-Reflection

1. In which of the virtues in the "beatitudes" in Matthew 5:1–11 do I most need to grow?

2. How can studying and focusing on Christ allow that to come about (2 Cor. 3:18)?

3. Which of the Key Lessons need more of my attention and why?
   _____
   _____
   _____

4. What do I enjoy most about or look most forward to, living as a Christian?
   _____
   _____
   _____

5. What are two or three action steps I need to take to progress in living as a Christian?
   _____
   _____
   _____

LESSON 13
Mission and Organization of the Church

Introduction

A CHURCH AS JESUS BUILDS it is not a building. It is not a human institution. Christ founded the church, and he is its builder. However, as Israel disobeyed God as his chosen people, so the church has also repeatedly been disobedient to him and corrupted Christ's design for the church. Humankind has as well failed to listen to the Word of God in other institutions God has established, such as the family, governments, and so forth. The church through the ages has too often seemingly lost its way in regard to the mission, organization, and vision Christ has for his church. Settling for "good" over "best," "permissible" over "desirable."

The church is designed to be the earthly manifestation of Christ himself—it is his body. It is also the temple of the Holy Spirit who dwells in and among God's people. The church was planned from the foundation of the world. It is the earthly manifestation of the kingdom of God, the kingdom that has already been established through Christ's mission but is still a work in progress.

However, because all humans sin and fall short of the glory of God, churches will also fall short of the glory of God. Thus disciples must neither expect nor demand perfection in themselves or their church communities. We must take great care in our judgments and criticisms of God's churches and their leaders. God has never dealt lightly with complaining, malcontented, and arrogant people—whether they are members or leaders. The reality is that God puts the parts in the body as he wills (1 Cor. 12:18). We must accept each member as a God-appointed part of the church, and treat all with respect, love, and with high regard (Rom. 12:10). This holds true even when practicing difficult types of church responsibilities that the Bible commands of us, such as discipline—rebuking, admonishing, and even excluding from the fellowship (2 Tim. 4:2–4; Tit. 3:10–11).

We each must "work out our salvation," that is, put in all the effort we can into growing in our faith and service to God. But we should work with a clear and constant understanding that God is working in all we think and do to accomplish his perfect will for his church as well as for each one of us (Phil. 2:12–13). We must believe that God places us in our church communities through our desires and our wills—that he wills and works within us for his purpose—and we must be careful when joining a church. We must be even more careful when considering leaving one. We must realize that God will not always send his servants where things are good and fun. He will sometimes send us to places where he needs us the most or where he wants us to be for our own sakes. This is especially true for mature Christians or those specifically called to leadership in Christian ministries. And those situations might not be particularly appealing or comfortable. Simply read the Book of Jonah or the Book of Acts to see this concept clearly illustrated in the lives of God's servants.

The purpose of this lesson is to explore this oft-maligned but God-established institution called the church.

Key Teaching: God gifts and appoints leaders in his church who are to lead, teach, and train the members in works of ministry.

1. Read Ephesians 4:11–13. Jesus appoints leaders to build and strengthen the church and its members. Consider the following:
   a. God has always worked through leaders. However, in the Western world where we emphasize individual freedoms (and to a lesser degree this is equally true elsewhere around the world) there is a gross tendency to disrespect, malign, and rebel against leaders just because they fail to do what we want them to. This rebellious tendency is very unwise and is not an attitude of Christ. A church that tolerates these attitudes will not flourish in Christ, and the body of believers should admonish members and leaders who are unchecked in their negative, rebellious attitudes, lest the offenders as well as the whole body stand in danger of discipline directly from God. How do you see this type of disrespect of leaders at every level in our society, be it government, education, social media, the church, our workplaces, and in our homes?

   _____
   _____
   _____

   b. Given all we have studied in this series about Christian attitude and conduct, how can we balance the need to be submissive to leaders with the responsibility to be wary of false prophet leaders?

   _____
   _____
   _____

   c. Read verse 11. The apostle Paul lists some specific kinds of leaders. Below I have included some definitions of each. Why do you suppose it is important for each disciple to know something about the kinds of leaders God appointed and used during Bible times?

   _____
   _____
   _____

      i. Apostle = one sent forth on a mission, an envoy, a delegate, a messenger, a herald.
         1. Christ specifically called the twelve original apostles, with their unique personal relationships to him, to establish the church (Mark 3:13–19), and thus this particular role must have ceased after a time, since these men were required to have seen the Lord and been called directly by Christ himself.
         2. Judas killed himself after his betrayal of Christ, and Matthias was selected to replace him (Acts 1:23–26).
         3. Jesus later directly called Saul of Tarsus who became the apostle Paul (Acts 9).
         4. Without going into detail, various scriptures indicate three general qualifications of apostles: to have been directly called by Christ or the Holy Spirit, to have seen the resurrected Lord, and to have the gift of performing miracles.
      ii. Prophet = a person gifted with divine truth
         1. Prophets were people called specifically by God through whom God would reveal specific truths. The term "prophet" is generally defined today as one who predicts the future, and

although prophets were often given knowledge of and messages concerning the future, their primary role was simply to deliver God's own messages.
2. Prophets were recognized as prophets by the church, since they were God appointed and inspired rather than appointed by the church. Prophets did by no means know all of God's truth, but were only given snippets of truths as the Holy Spirit willed.
   iii. Evangelist = a bearer of good news, a preacher of the gospel. Evangelists such as Timothy and Titus were given more comprehensive ministries in establishing churches, appointing church leaders, administering church discipline, and teaching and protecting the truth of Christ.
   iv. Pastor = a shepherd, a feeder, a protector of a flock. Curiously, this particular word is used only once in the New Testament in the aforementioned scripture, however, it has become a catchall "title" for many key church leaders.
   v. Teacher = an instructor. This simply designates one who is able to teach. In early times, teachers may have been given directly from the Holy Spirit a gift of specific knowledge, or they may have learned it from one of the apostles or other leaders.

d. In New Testament times, there were sometimes overlap in these roles. Apostles variously acted as prophets, evangelists, pastors, and teachers. Prophets might also be evangelists, pastors, and teachers. Evangelists might also have been prophets, pastors and teachers. But in reading the New Testament that inclusion seemingly often did not work upward. Many teachers were not considered pastors as far as the role was concerned. Many pastors were not considered evangelists, prophets, and so forth. Why is studying to understand the various roles and responsibilities of the church's first leaders important for the church today to be effectively led?

_____

_____

_____

e. Consider also other types of leaders and leadership designations the various churches of the New Testament employed. A few simplified definitions follow.
   i. Elder = in scripture it signifies older males recognized as leaders of a clan, group, or church; in first-century Israel a committee of elders oversaw the various communities; Paul appointed elders in the churches that he started (Acts 14:23).
   ii. Shepherd = a leader or guide of a group; Israel had a long history of shepherding and was very familiar with the role of shepherds out in the field as well as in communities.
   iii. Bishop = a superintendent or overseer.
   iv. Note: Elders, shepherds, pastors, and bishops were arguably designations for the same leadership roles in the early church
   v. Deacon = a minister or servant; the deacons of the New Testament were seemingly appointed for specific tasks, ministries, and responsibilities.
   vi. Priest = an intermediary offering sacrifices to God for others; this title for individual leaders is not used in the New Testament, as the New Testament asserts the priesthood of all believers with Jesus as the High Priest (1 Pet. 2:9); a "priesthood," however, was developed in some churches over the first few hundred years and is still in existence in some.

f. What types of religious leaders are you most familiar with?
    _____
    _____

g. What have been your general attitudes toward church leaders, and what kinds of attitude corrections might be in order for you?
    _____
    _____

h. Do you consider your experiences with religious leaders to be generally positive or negative? Why so?
    _____
    _____

i. Because of variety across churches and denominations in all their varied cultural contexts, all kinds of leadership positions exist. These variations can certainly cause problems but perhaps also serve to help the church adapt and survive in a fallen and ever-changing world. How do you see variation in churches as a potential overall strength, and how do you see it as a potential weakness?
    _____
    _____

j. Consider these thoughts and observations. Based on your present perceptions or beliefs, note whether you generally agree or disagree with each practice.
    i. Like human families, churches may operate independently, to varying degrees but remain effectively interdependent in the kingdom of God.
        _____
        _____

    ii. Organized denominations also operate differently in terms of how much control is exercised over individual leaders and congregations.
        _____
        _____

    iii. Some churches follow their church's tradition in regard to leadership without questioning the tradition's origin and purpose, feeling it is their church's right and prerogative to determine their leadership structure, and so forth.
        _____
        _____

    iv. Some churches have designated leadership roles based on what they see as the "correct" roles emerging from scripture and feel these should be the only recognized leadership roles in every church.
        _____
        _____
        _____

v. Others believe in varying degrees in "freedom of forms" with regard to leadership, which means they may adapt these scriptural roles to their own needs and culture.

k. One thing for certain is that God has given us numerous leadership principles that come directly from his own personality and purposes. He surely expects these to be regarded and obeyed, regardless of the type of positions or roles we may define within our individual communities and denominations.
  i. Leaders will be judged more strictly than members (James 3:1).
  ii. Leaders must lead as servants not as rulers (Matt. 20:25–28).
  iii. Leaders and churches must be careful about promoting honorific titles and not merely humble positions of service (Matt. 23:1–12).
  iv. Leaders must be good examples in life and in teaching (Matt. 7:15–20; 1 Tim. 4:11–16; Heb. 13:7).

l. Paul commands all Christians to submit to each other, which includes members submitting to leaders and leaders "submitting" to members (Eph. 5:21).
  i. God expects all Christians to be generally submissive to him and to one another from the inside out (Matt. 5:3–12, 38–42).
  ii. Jesus instructs us to lead as servants (thus submissively) not as tyrants (Matt. 20:24–28).
  iii. We are given instructions to be submissive, basically until we can no longer submit *and* still be in obedience to God.
  iv. Unless we are in a controlling, corrupt church, going against church leadership should be an exception for us, not the rule or general pattern. Review these passages concerning Christian character and behavior and how each weighs upon our respect for leaders. Summarize what is expected then of individual Christians.
  v. Be submissive to and honor one another (Eph. 5:21; Rom. 12:10)

  vi. Imitate the faith of and obey your church leaders (Heb. 13:7–17)

  vii. Be meek or humble to all (Matt. 5:5; Phil. 2:1–8)

  viii. Be submissive to secular governments (Rom. 13:1–2)

    ix. Be submissive in marriage (Eph. 5:22, 25)

    x. Children be submissive to parents (Eph. 6:1–3; Deut. 5:16)

m. Consider these passages about leaders, and in your own words summarize the implication for Christians.
    i. Do not lead in a controlling way, as leaders in the world do, but rather lead as "the least, the last and the worst," so to speak (Matt. 20:25–28; 1 Cor. 15:9; 1 Tim. 1:15; 1 Cor. 4:9).

    ii. Preach the gospel, correcting, rebuking, encouraging, and training (2 Tim. 3:16–4:4).

    iii. Shepherd the flock under your care (1 Pet. 5:1–7).

    iv. Do not let anyone look down on you because you are young, rather be exemplary to everyone (1 Tim. 4:12).

    v. Encourage and rebuke with authority (Tit. 2:15).

    vi. Do not let anyone despise your authority (Tit. 2:15).

    vii. What do you think it means for someone to despise a leader's authority?

Key Teaching: The church is a fellowship, or partnership, for the collective purpose of carrying out God's will within the church and in the world itself.

1. Read Acts 2:42. List the four key things the believers were said to have devoted themselves to, and what each means or looked like practically?
    a. _____
    b. _____
    c. _____
    d. _____
    e. _____

2. Read Acts 2:42–47. As previously explained, the "fellowship" is an all-encompassing lifestyle, and this needs to be clearly understood in order for a believer to function well in the church. Unlike the modern use of the word "fellowship," which most often merely refers to socializing or fraternizing, the word used in the original Greek language, *koinonia*, means "a partnership."
    a. Although not always translated as fellowship from the Greek, the word *koinonia* is used to describe this partnership among members. Though this list is not by any means exhaustive, consider these examples. Mark which of these that you have observed or heard about in churches and briefly describe how it occurred?
        i. Sharing of spiritual relationships in Christ (Acts 2:42; 1 John 1:3).
        _____
        ii. Financial assistance between churches (Rom. 15:26; 2 Cor. 9:13).
        _____
        iii. Sharing of physical resources within the church (Acts 2:44–45; 4:32).
        _____

iv. As a participation in or communion (Lord's Supper) with the body of Christ (1 Cor. 10:16).

v. Mutual support in the church's mission of outreach and evangelism (2 Cor. 8:4; Phil. 1:5).

vi. As a mutual communion through the Holy Spirit (2 Cor. 13:14).

vii. The mutual participation in Christ's suffering (Phil. 1:27–30; 3:10).

viii. The mutual sharing of, or partnership in, the faith (Philem. 6).

b. In a partnership, the relationship of the partners is based on a common mission, purpose, values, and goals. Why is this essential to an effective partnership?

c. In a partnership, the mission and purpose of the partnership comes before personal or selfish interests of the partners. Also mission drives organization, not the other way around as happens in many institutional bureaucracies. What happens to the effectiveness of a community that is more concerned with organization and such than it is about its mission?

d. In a partnership, partners have roles and are expected to contribute equally. What happens when a partner does not contribute to the mission of the partnership?

3. Participation in the fellowship is a very serious part of a Christian's life. The Bible equates the failure to be a functioning part of an assembly of believers to a departure from Christ himself, and it reserves some harsh warnings for those who neglect it.

a. Read Hebrews 10:19–39 and consider the various admonitions and warnings that scripture gives to these Christians concerning personal commitment to God, mutual support among members, and the neglecting of the assemblies of the church.

   i. Note how their waning faith is reflected in their waning participation. How do you see a connection between a strong faith in Christ and a devoted participation in the church?

   ii. Next, notice how their waning participation is equated with intentionally living in sin. What connection is there between neglect of the fellowship and intentionally going back to our old lifestyles?

   iii. Lastly, notice what the text says those deserve who go back to their old lifestyles.

   iv. After reading the seriousness of these warnings, how do you see the modern church and Christians that treat church attendance and participation haphazardly, both in attitude and action? Explain your answer.

   v. What does this have to say of the often-heard idea of people saying they are Christians but by their own choices are not a part of the fellowship or church?

4. Individual churches or congregations are a part of the universal church and share in its fellowship and mission. Consider these statements, and after each principle make a note of why it is important.
   a. It is God who determines who is in the body of Christ, the church. Entrance into it is based on his salvation, which flows from his own grace and his inclusion of individuals in the body of Christ.

   b. No church has a human or organizational monopoly on access to God or the sole right to be in his church.

c. It is God himself who adds new members to his fellowship, the church (Acts 2:47).

d. God places the parts (members) in the church where he wills them to be (1 Cor. 12:18).

e. It is the Holy Spirit that baptizes us into the body of Christ (1 Cor. 12:13).

f. It is God, and God *only*, who knows without any questions those who truly belong to him (2 Tim. 2:19).

g. No one can come to Jesus unless called and allowed by God to come (John 6:44).

h. No one can confess "Jesus is Lord" but by the right given by the Holy Spirit (1 Cor. 12:3).

i. It is not the business of a church or a disciple to uproot, dislodge, or cut down those who even *look* like Jesus's people (Matt. 13:24–30).

j. When we participate in the Lord's Supper, we are commanded to examine the body of Christ. This is not about picturing Jesus hanging on the cross for our sins. In communion, we must also picture the body of Christ as referring to his church. When we partake of this Holy Communion, we must remember and acknowledge the body of Christ, not only in our local setting, but wherever it may exist—even if we have serious disagreements on various doctrinal points. Why do many people go to the church service and then see each activity as all about their own connections to God, rather than being there to give encouragement to the others, participate with all in each activity, and draw near in more intimate fellowship?

k. Special note: There will be times when fellowship may not be possible or may have to be limited because of various doctrinal and practical issues. But a proper attitude toward fellowship begins and ends with a humble heart. God will certainly know if any one of us has a divisive, prideful, "I am right" spirit, and he will resist it. If we err, let us err on the side of mercy toward one another and toward the world in general. This is how Jesus wanted it, saying, "I desire mercy…" (Matt. 9:13).

l. In your own words, how do you think that we individually, as well as collectively in our local church families, can participate more effectively in the universal or worldwide church, in our attitudes and in our actions?

Key Teaching: The Holy Spirit unifies the church in Christ, and Jesus is the bond that holds the church together.

1. Jesus is the bond of peace that holds his church together (Eph. 2:14). Make a note about what each of these passages means. Jesus made clear to the apostles the essentiality of every disciple to be and remain "in him" (John 15:1–9).
    a. In Christ every spiritual blessing is to be found (Eph. 1:3).

    b. In Christ we have been adopted by God the Father, he has forgiven us, and we find our eternal purpose (Eph. 1:4–12).

    c. In Christ we are sealed with the Holy Spirit when we become believers (Eph. 1:13–14).

    d. It is in Christ that we find spiritual enlightenment of the hope, riches, and power we have as believers (Eph. 1:15–21).

    e. Christ is the ruler over everything and is the head of his church (Eph. 1:22–23).

f. When we are born again, we are raised from death and are seated with him in the heavenly or spiritual realms so that he can show through us the riches of his grace through the kindness he shows us in Christ Jesus (Eph. 2:1–7).

g. We are saved by his grace when we come to faith in him, and there is no way that we can earn or merit a single ounce of grace. Grace is and will forever be, by its own definition, purely a gift from God (Eph. 2:8–9).

h. We are, however, recreated by Christ in order to do good works on his behalf (Eph. 2:10).

i. It is in him that God breaks down all the walls that stand between us as unbelievers, even the most formidable ones like that which stood between Jews and Gentiles. He is the church's "superglue"—"the bond of peace"—that holds us together. It is only through our ironclad commitments to him that we can find the deepest unity—the kind that supersedes all our other differences (Eph. 2:11–18; 4:3).

j. In Christ, then, we collectively comprise God's household built on the foundation Christ laid in and through the apostles (Eph. 2:19–29).

k. In Christ the church has grown to be a dwelling or temple for God on earth through his Holy Spirit, and each believer is made a part of it by God himself (Eph. 2:21–22).

2. True Christian unity is of the Holy Spirit (Eph. 4:3–6). Make a note or two for each of these statements about the implication of being unified in the body.
   a. We are given the Holy Spirit when we are saved and added to the body of Christ (Eph. 2:13–14; Gal. 3:26–4:7).

b. The Spirit unifies us in the body, and it is the responsibility of each of us to maintain this unity, first in our own hearts, and then, as far is it lies within us, among all the members of Christ's body (Eph. 4:3).

c. In fact, God wants us to make every effort to maintain the unity the Spirit established in us
   i. by living a life worthy of our calling by the gospel (Eph. 4:1; Phil. 1:27). In this context, what does this mean and what does it have to do with unity in the body of Christ?

   ii. by being completely humble, gentle, patient, forbearing, and loving (Eph. 4:2).

Key Teaching: God gives all members of the body of Christ the general gifts of discipleship and service, but he also gives particular gifts to various individual members. All the gifts are given for serving and building up the body.

1. Every member must live in imitation of Christ and follow the example of the apostles as well as those of other Christians and leaders around us who follow Christ (1 Cor. 11:1).
   a. The apostle Paul taught Christians to imitate him. Jesus said it was by one's fruit that you would know them (Matt. 7:15–20). What kind of fruit—good and bad—should you look for in order to test the fruit of those who lead you and whom you might imitate?

   b. Imitating other Christians is good, but only to the degree that they imitate Christ (1 Cor. 11:1). How can we make sure that ultimately we are imitating Jesus and not merely other people?

2. Members are given specific gifts to use in the body (Rom. 12:3–8 and 1 Cor. 12:4–7). A gift represents a particular talent, natural or spiritual, unlearned or learned, that God gives us the opportunity and the responsibility to use. *Every Christian* has the gift of being a disciple and all that implies. However, some will prove even more capable in basic or specialized Christian activities and ministries. The natural gifts and abilities that we have, even before we are saved, when consecrated by the Holy Spirit, will generally prove useful in the body as well.
   a. If you are already a Christian, what gifts do you already contribute to the body?

b. If you are not yet a Christian, what natural or innate gifts do you think you might already have to contribute to the body?

c. How do you think God views individuals who fail to use their gifts, abilities, and resources to serve the church?

Key Teaching: In the church, every member belongs to all of the others and is thus expected to be submissive, participative, and generous toward others in the church.

1. As members of the body of Christ, we are connected and are essential to one another (1 Cor. 12:18–27).
    a. Why is functioning in this kind of interconnectedness difficult for us today?

    b. What can we do to guard against any "disconnectedness" in our own church life?

2. In the body of Christ, members belong to one another (Rom. 12:4–5).
    a. What do you think it means that we "belong" to each other, and how does this apply to our lives as members of the body?

    b. In view of what you know about Christ and the scriptures, what do you think should be the limits to and controls placed on this principle?

Key Teaching: The church has been given Christ's mission, the "Great Commission," and every member must accept this overarching purpose and participate accordingly.

1. As disciples living in imitation of Christ, his mission is our mission.
    a. Read Luke 19:10 and Matthew 4:19. What did Jesus say he came here for?

b. Further, what did he say he would make us into if we followed him?

___

c. Read Matthew 20:28. What did Jesus say he came for, and how do you think this supports the Great Commission?

___

2. As the church collectively, we have thus been entrusted with Christ's mission and ministry. Read 2 Corinthians 5:16–21 and consider these questions.
    a. What does it mean that Jesus has entrusted his ministry to us?

    ___

    b. What does it mean to be an ambassador for Christ in our world (look up the definition of the word "ambassador" and perhaps do a little research on what ambassadors to other countries actually do)?

    ___

3. For the body to function as Christ intends, each member must do her or his part (Eph. 4:16).
    a. Consider the scripture referenced here. What do you think the body will look like when any of us fail to do our part?

    ___

    b. Why do you suppose many don't participate in church communities beyond casual church attendance?

    ___

Key Teaching: The church is a family, and its members are expected by God to conduct themselves appropriately.

1. We must learn how to conduct ourselves in the household of God (1 Tim. 3:14–15).
    a. What do you think it means concerning "how to conduct ourselves properly in God's household"? Is this only talking about when we are in a church service or church building, as some might surmise, or does it extend out into our daily lives? What do you think?

    ___

b. Based on what you have learned so far, list a few general "conducts" that scripture teaches us are critical behaviors for each church member?

2. Church membership is a gift and an honor, not a right or an entitlement (John 15:1–8).
   a. Who is the vine we are to be attached to?

   b. How do we stay attached to him?

   c. What happens if we fail to stay well attached to him?

   d. Who is it that decides what branches are unfruitful and thus need removed?

   e. What is the outcome of branches that he removes?

   f. How can we behave in such a way so as not to have to fear being removed?

Self-Reflection

1. Why must I as a disciple be an active, involved member of a local church community?

2. How have I been concerning church involvement so far in my life? What obstacles are in the way of me getting involved? What excuses do I make for not being involved, and how do I believe God sees these?

3. Based on what I have learned up to now, how should I pick a church to be a part of?
   _____
   _____

4. How should I pick leaders to follow (often this is done by picking a church to be a part of)?
   _____
   _____

5. Which of the key teachings in this lesson apply most to me at this point?
   _____
   _____

6. Which teachings do I have more questions about and need to ask questions about or do more research on?
   _____
   _____
   _____

Conclusion
Moving Forward

As was stated in the beginning, trying to put together a study that will truly help others discover Jesus through a study of the scripture is most formidable. This series is by no means exhaustive, although those who complete it may feel it has been exhausting. The study will be useless or even counterproductive if effort is not made consistently over time to put what is learned into practice and to continue seeking Jesus as well through the revelation of his creation, the guidance of the Holy Spirit, and participation in the body of Christ, the church.

James said it this way:

Do not merely listen to the word, and so deceive yourselves. Do what it says. Anyone who listens to the word but does not do what it says is like someone who looks at his face in a mirror and, after looking at himself, goes away and immediately forgets what he looks like. But whoever looks intently into the perfect law that gives freedom, and continues in it—not forgetting what they have heard, but doing it—they will be blessed in what they do. (James 1:22–25)

This outline of study is intended to give the seeker a thorough start in understanding the breadth and depth of the scriptures. These are the scriptures that "breathe out" Jesus from the beginning to end. He was in the beginning. He created the world. He died to save the world. He will finally redeem the world he made. He sustains it daily by his powerful Word. Jesus is Lord. He has all authority in heaven and on earth. It is before him that everyone will bow, now or later. Everyone, without exception, will one day bow to Jesus.

Jesus is the Word of God. He is the exact representation of the beauty and glory of God. Jesus is life. Jesus is the light of the world. Jesus is the way to God. Jesus is the truth of God. Jesus is the personified love of God. He is the artist behind the beauty and magnificence we see daily. He was there at our beginning, he is here now, and he will be there to meet us at the end. He is the author and perfecter of our faith. As he sought us, he desires we seek him and reach out and find him. He wants a relationship with each of us.

When we have discovered Jesus, we have discovered the *one* thing—the important thing. It cannot be stolen from us. We need Jesus Christ more than we need our next breath. We need him more than we need food or water. We need him more than we need a place to live. We need him more than any other person or thing! He is more loving than humans can comprehend. His power is incomparable. His grace is immeasurable. His beauty is indescribable. He is the summation of all that is lovely and beautiful because he is its creator.

In this present age, he may seem to be unbelievable. Jesus, however, is real. He has manifested himself on earth already. He showed himself as resurrected with "convincing proofs." He will come again to take those who have found him and trusted him to be with him forever in his redeemed realm, the place he has prepared for those who love him. This study is a meager but best effort at what has been described as a most formidable challenge—to help others discover Jesus. But we walk by faith and not by sight—not by sight yet, anyway. This outline of study is written in the hope that perhaps at least a few will discover Jesus through it and that many others will be enriched in their relationships with him and with each other!

I conclude with these beautiful words of the apostle Paul: "Now to him who is able to do immeasurably more than all we ask or imagine, according to his power that is at work within us, to him be glory in the church and in Christ Jesus throughout all generations, for ever and ever! Amen" (Eph. 3:20-21).

Made in the USA
Columbia, SC
13 March 2025